B. C.
DIP IN ROAD

Johnny Hart

FAWCETT GOLD MEDAL • NEW YORK

B.C. DIP IN ROAD

Copyright © 1969 by Publishers Newspaper Syndicate

Copyright © 1974 by CBS Publications, The Consumer Publishing Division of CBS Inc.

Published by Fawcett Gold Medal Books, a unit of CBS Publications, the Consumer Publishing Division of CBS Inc., by special arrangement with Publishers-Hall Syndicate, Inc.

ISBN: 0-449-13678-7

Printed in the United States of America

23   22   21   20   19

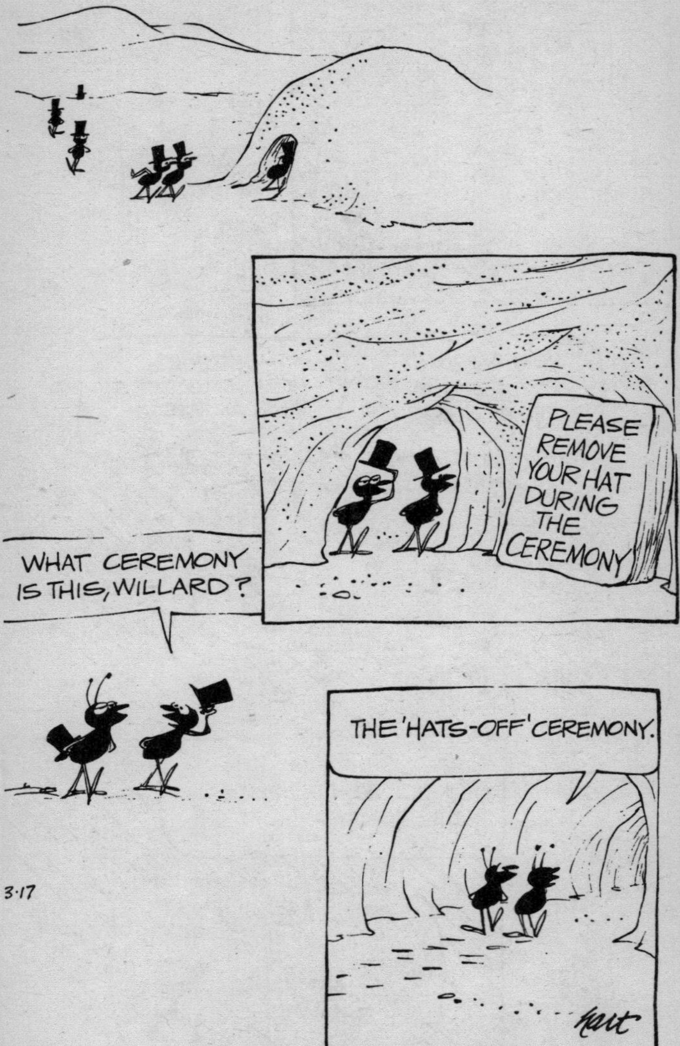
PLEASE REMOVE YOUR HAT DURING THE CEREMONY
WHAT CEREMONY IS THIS, WILLARD?
THE 'HATS-OFF' CEREMONY.
3·17
hart

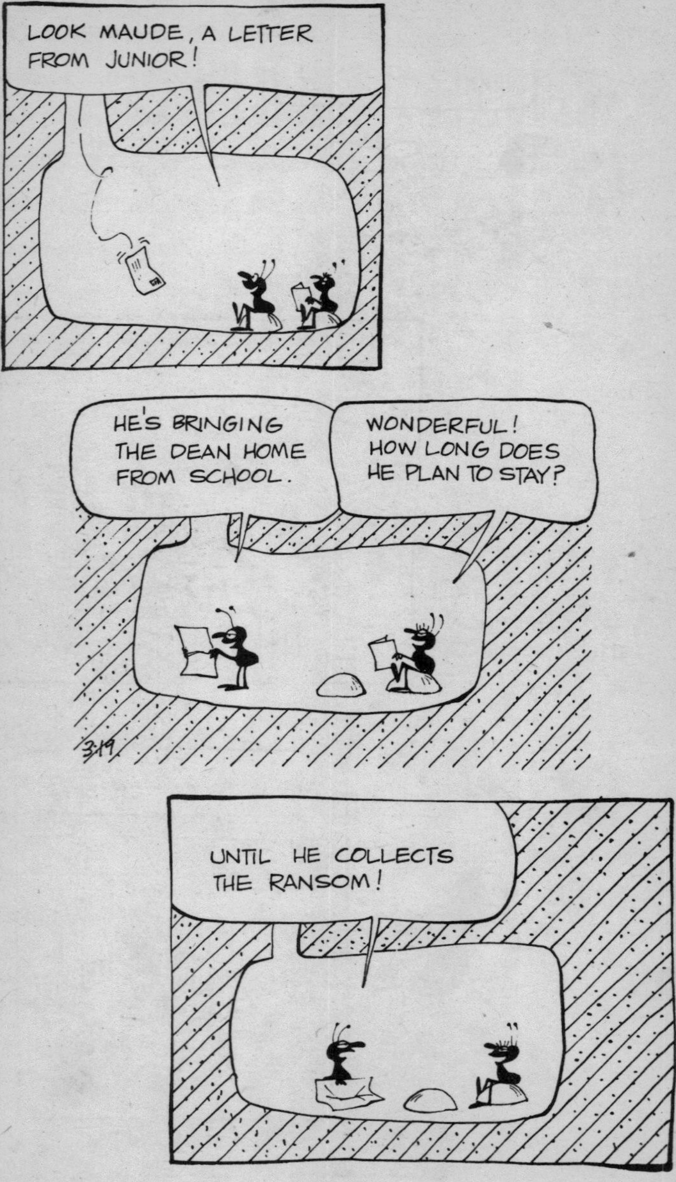
LOOK MAUDE, A LETTER FROM JUNIOR!
HE'S BRINGING THE DEAN HOME FROM SCHOOL.
WONDERFUL! HOW LONG DOES HE PLAN TO STAY?
3-19
UNTIL HE COLLECTS THE RANSOM!

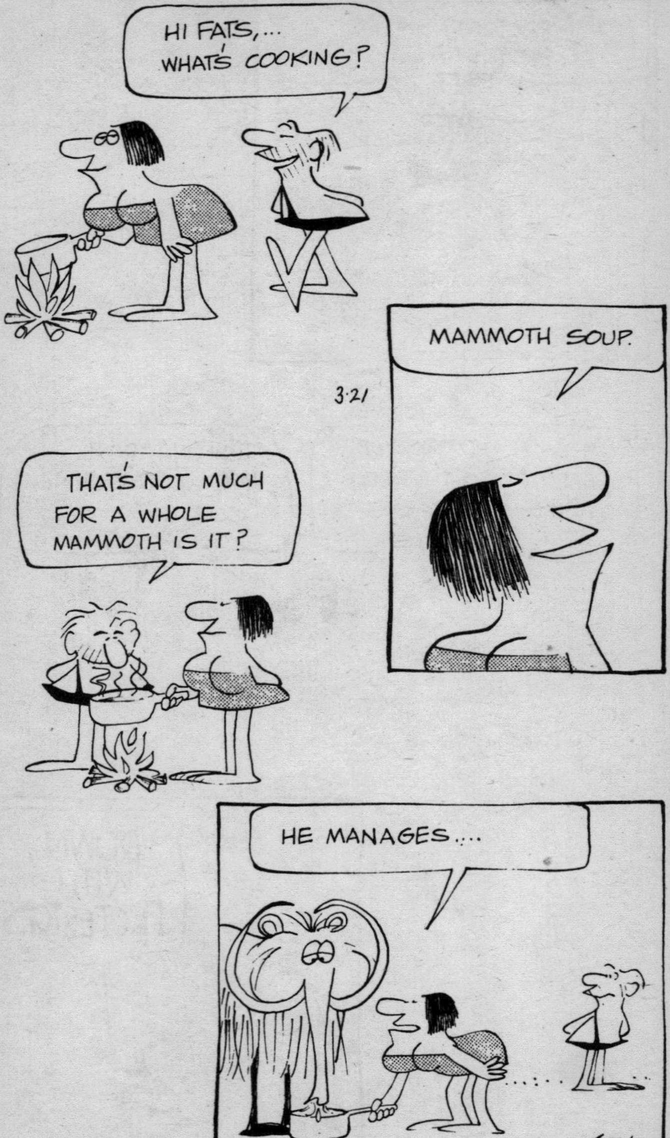
HI FATS,...
WHAT'S COOKING?
MAMMOTH SOUP.
3·21
THAT'S NOT MUCH
FOR A WHOLE
MAMMOTH IS IT?
HE MANAGES....
hart

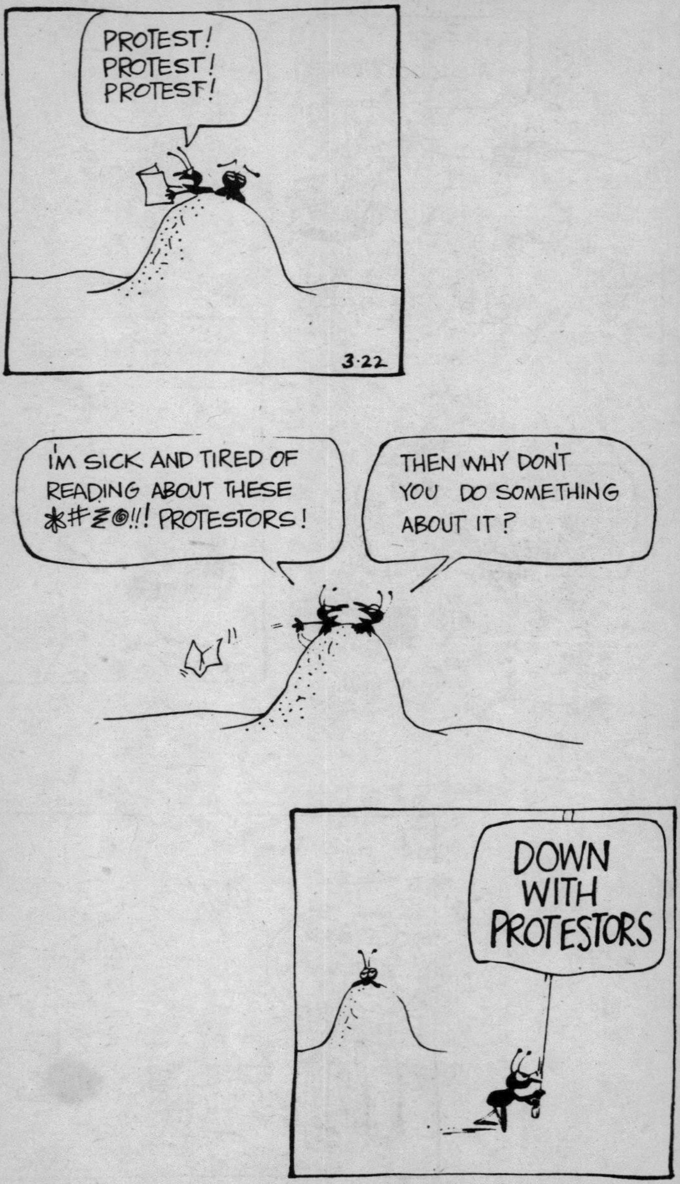
PROTEST! PROTEST! PROTEST!
3·22
I'M SICK AND TIRED OF READING ABOUT THESE *#≹@!!! PROTESTORS!
THEN WHY DON'T YOU DO SOMETHING ABOUT IT?
DOWN WITH PROTESTORS

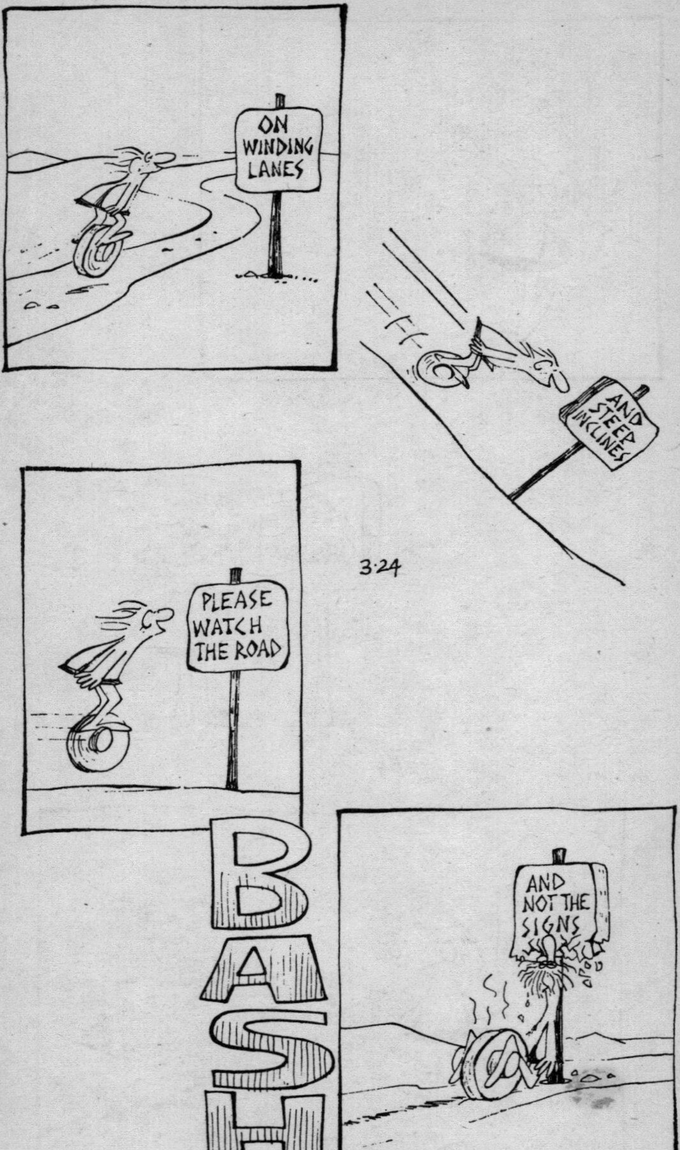
ON WINDING LANES
AND STEEP INCLINES
3·24
PLEASE WATCH THE ROAD
BASH
AND NOT THE SIGNS

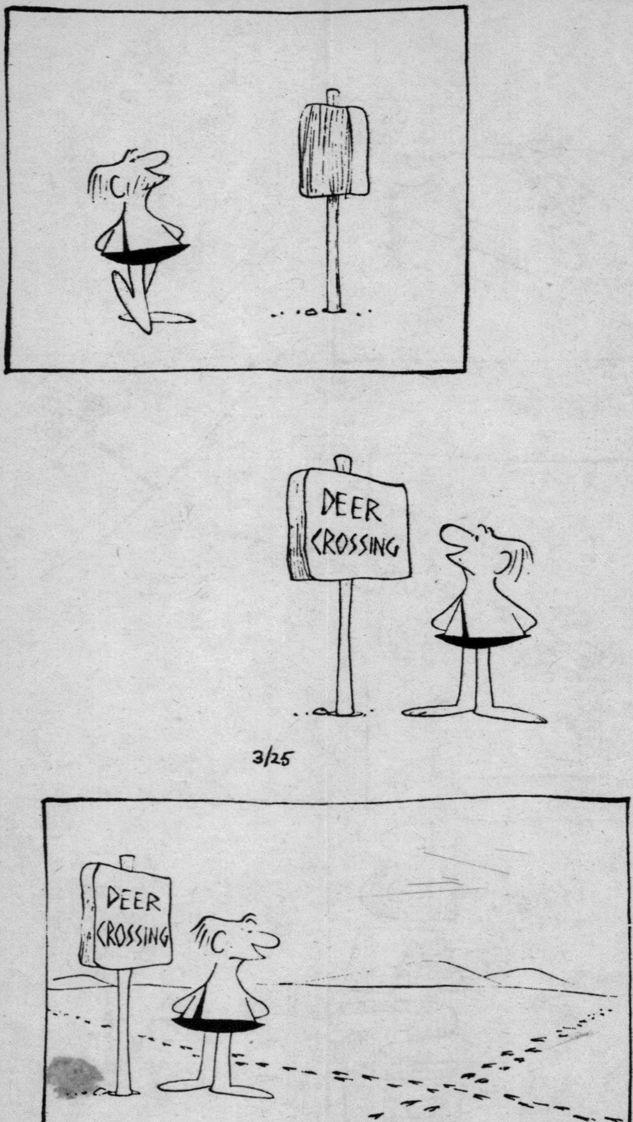
DEER CROSSING
3/25
DEER CROSSING

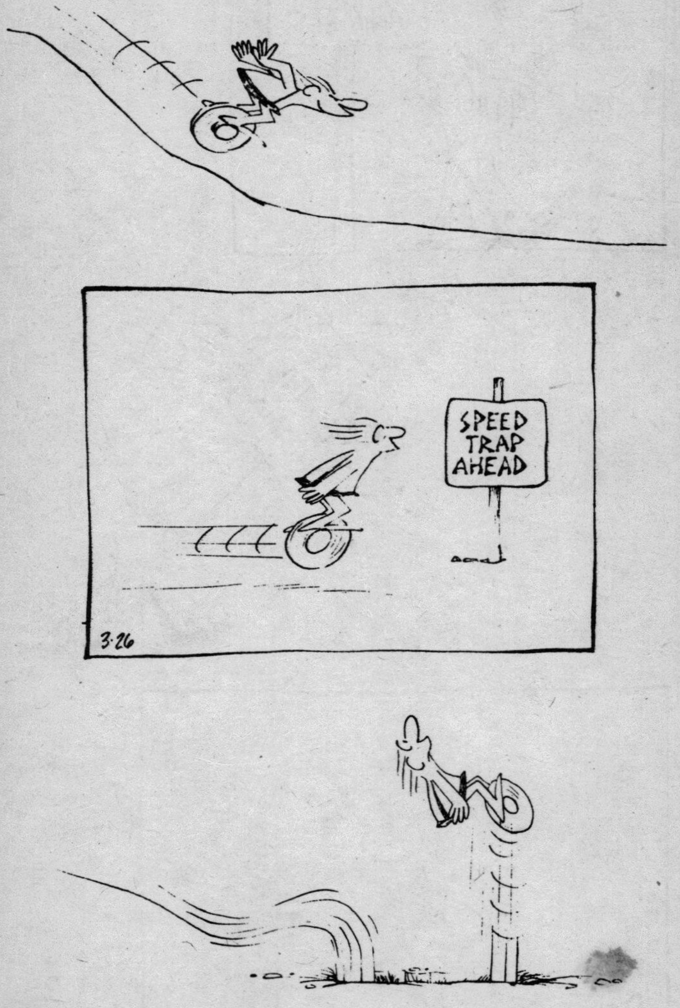
SPEED
TRAP
AHEAD
3·26
hart

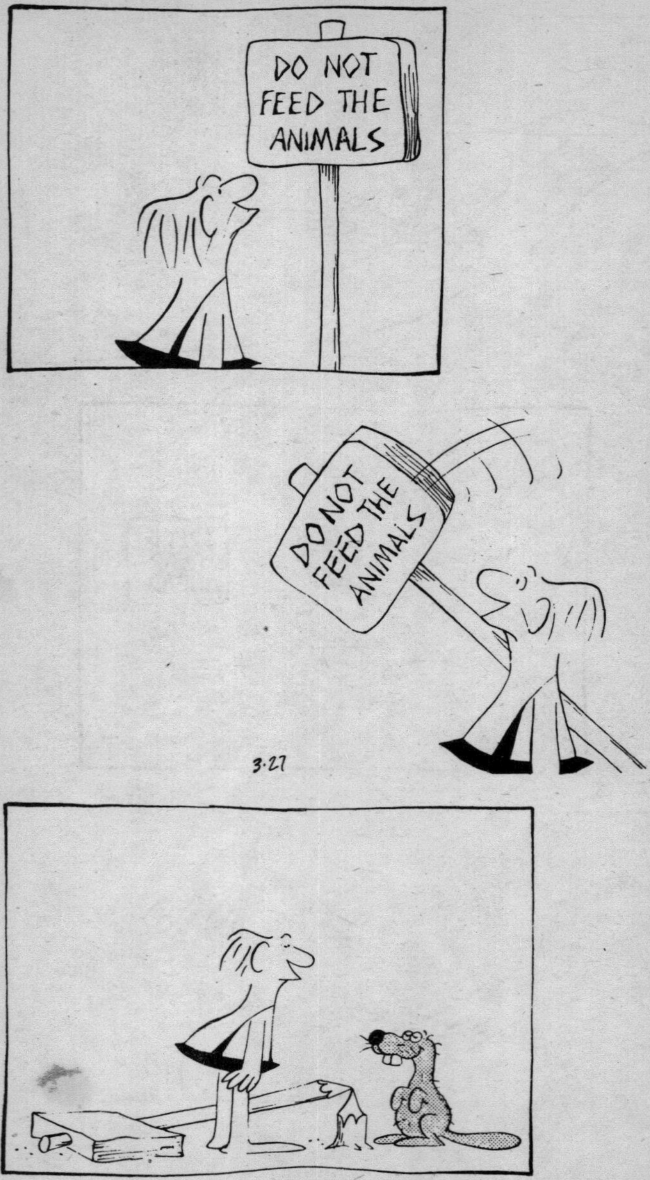
DO NOT FEED THE ANIMALS
DO NOT FEED THE ANIMALS
3·27

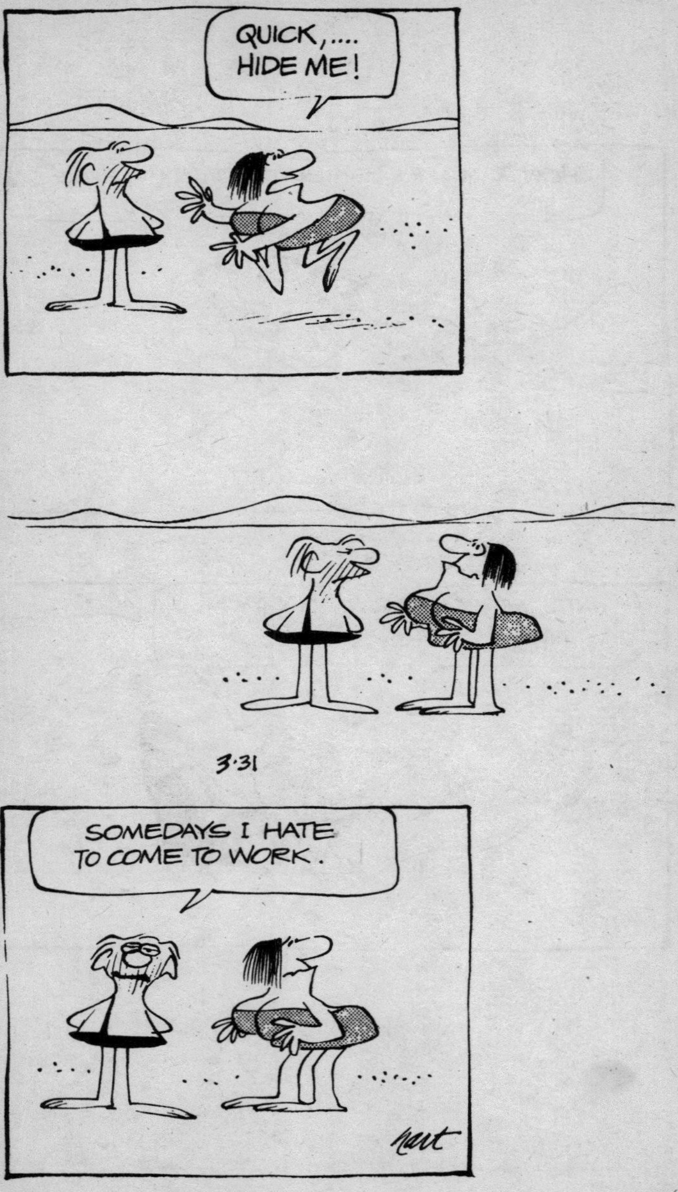
QUICK, ...
HIDE ME!
3·31
SOMEDAYS I HATE
TO COME TO WORK.
hart

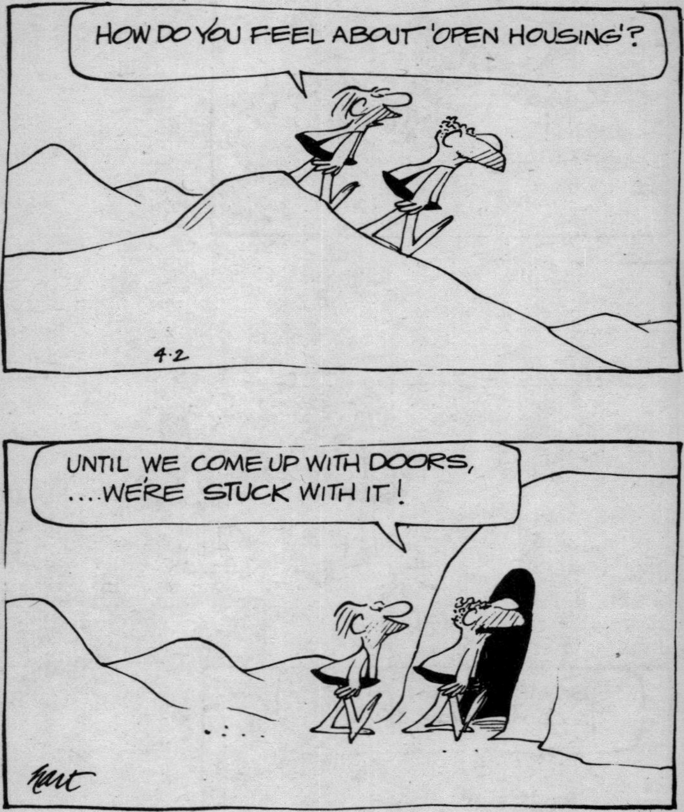
HOW DO YOU FEEL ABOUT 'OPEN HOUSING'?
4·2
UNTIL WE COME UP WITH DOORS, ...WE'RE STUCK WITH IT!
hart

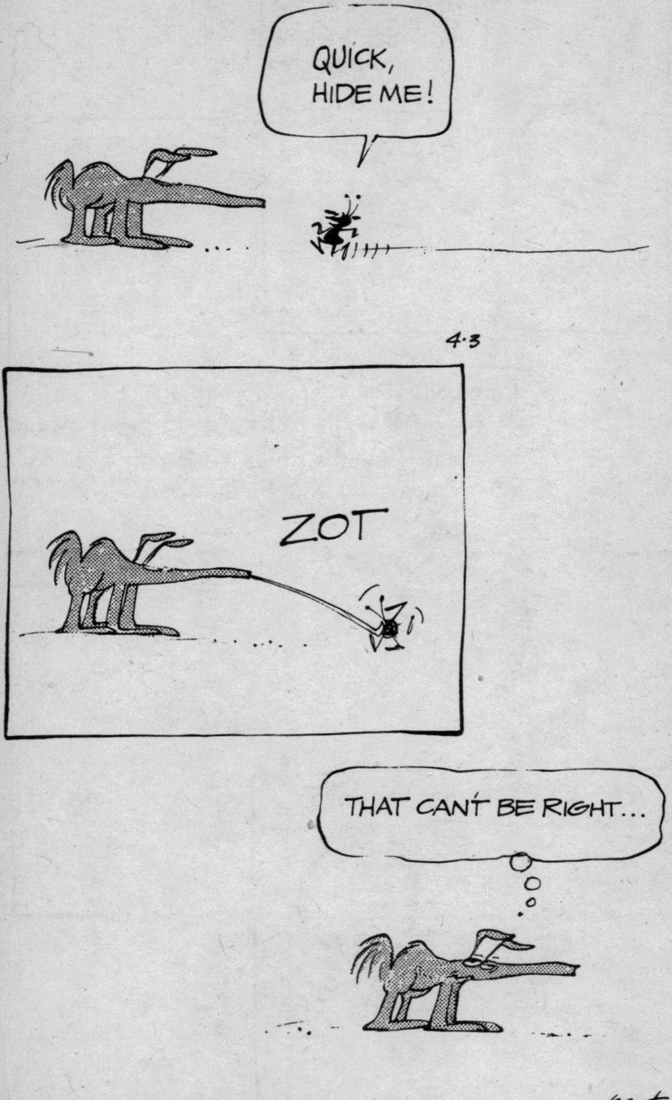
QUICK, HIDE ME!
4·3
ZOT
THAT CAN'T BE RIGHT...
hart

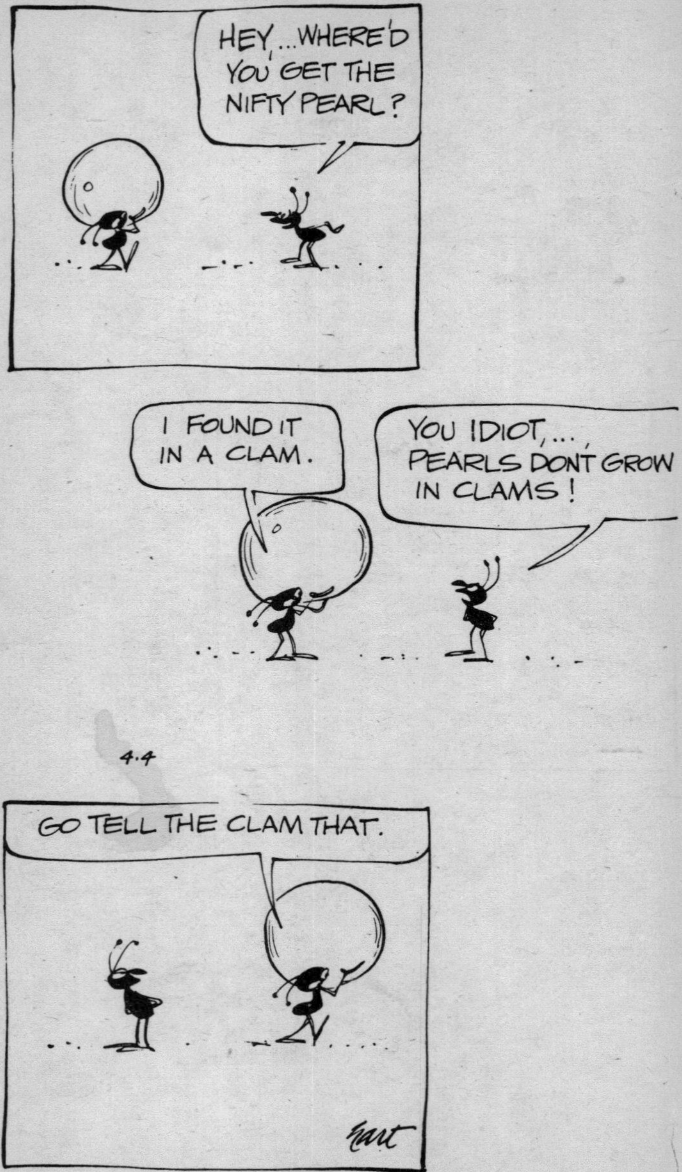
HEY,...WHERE'D YOU GET THE NIFTY PEARL?
I FOUND IT IN A CLAM.
YOU IDIOT,...,
PEARLS DONT GROW IN CLAMS!
4.4
GO TELL THE CLAM THAT.
hart

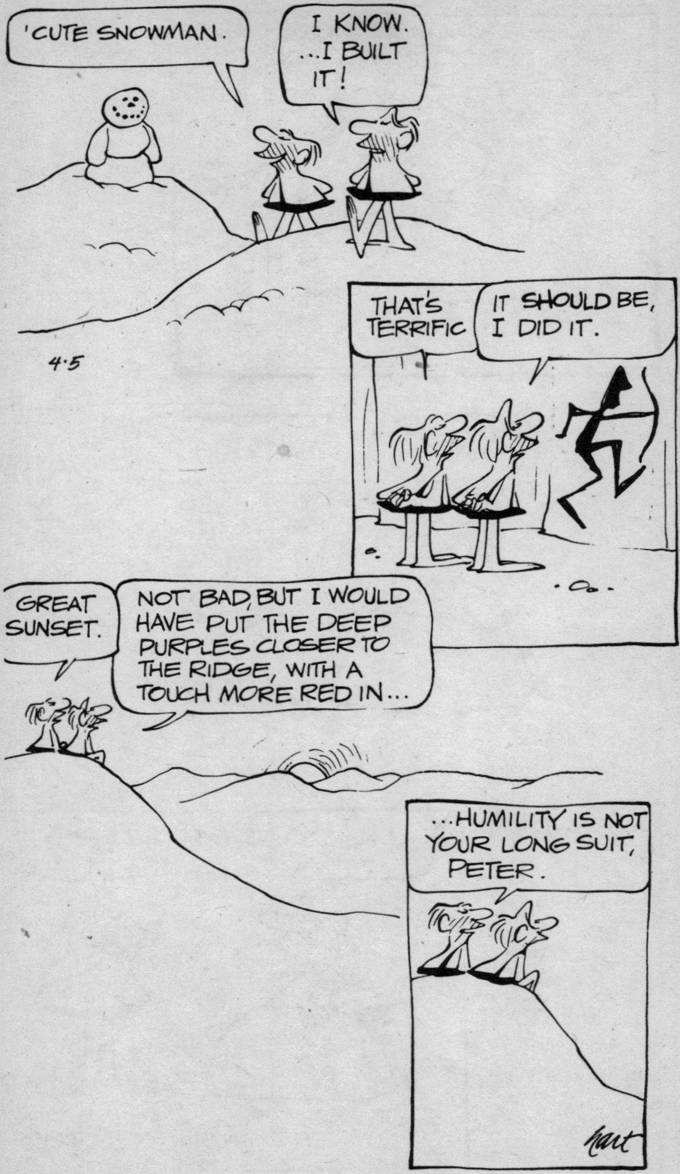
'CUTE SNOWMAN.
I KNOW. ...I BUILT IT!
4·5
THAT'S TERRIFIC
IT SHOULD BE, I DID IT.
GREAT SUNSET.
NOT BAD, BUT I WOULD HAVE PUT THE DEEP PURPLES CLOSER TO THE RIDGE, WITH A TOUCH MORE RED IN...
...HUMILITY IS NOT YOUR LONG SUIT, PETER.
hart

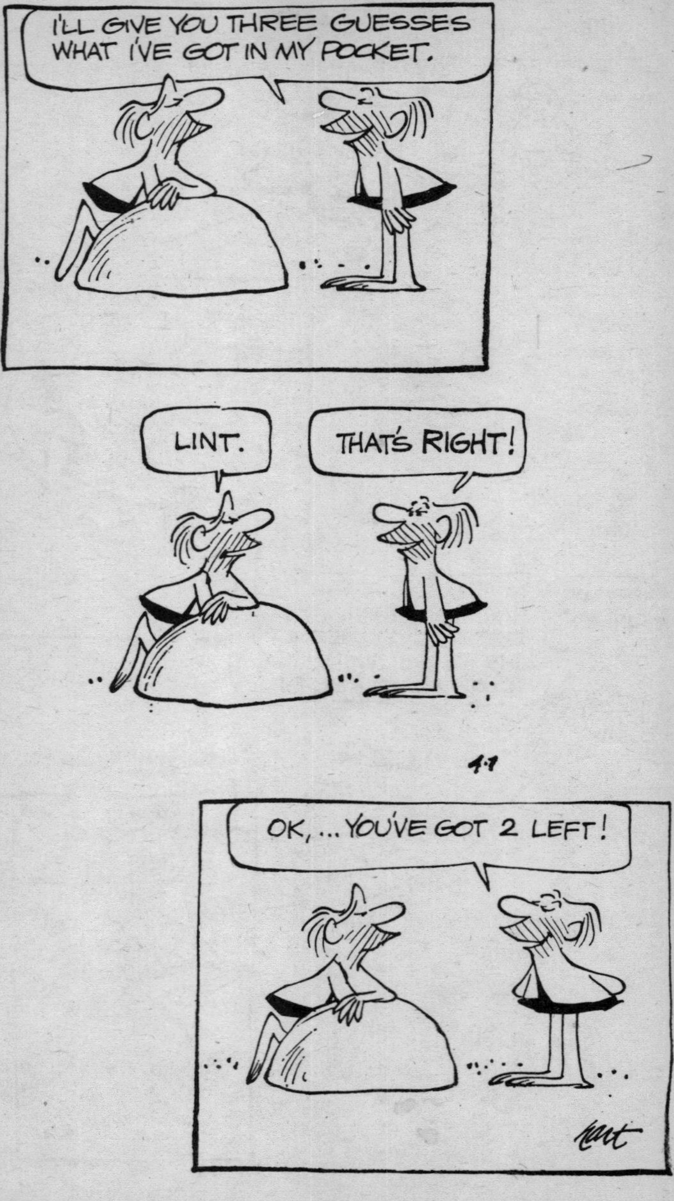
I'LL GIVE YOU THREE GUESSES WHAT I'VE GOT IN MY POCKET.
LINT.
THAT'S RIGHT!
OK, ... YOU'VE GOT 2 LEFT!

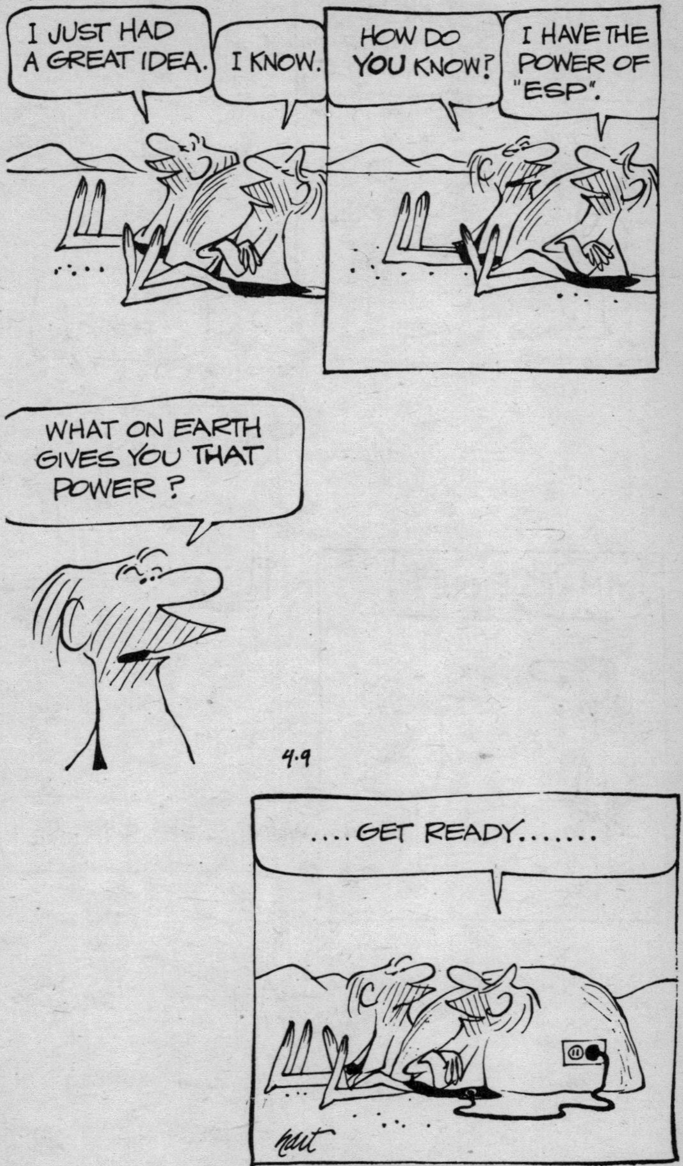
I JUST HAD A GREAT IDEA.
I KNOW.
HOW DO YOU KNOW?
I HAVE THE POWER OF "ESP".
WHAT ON EARTH GIVES YOU THAT POWER ?
4·9
....GET READY.......
hart

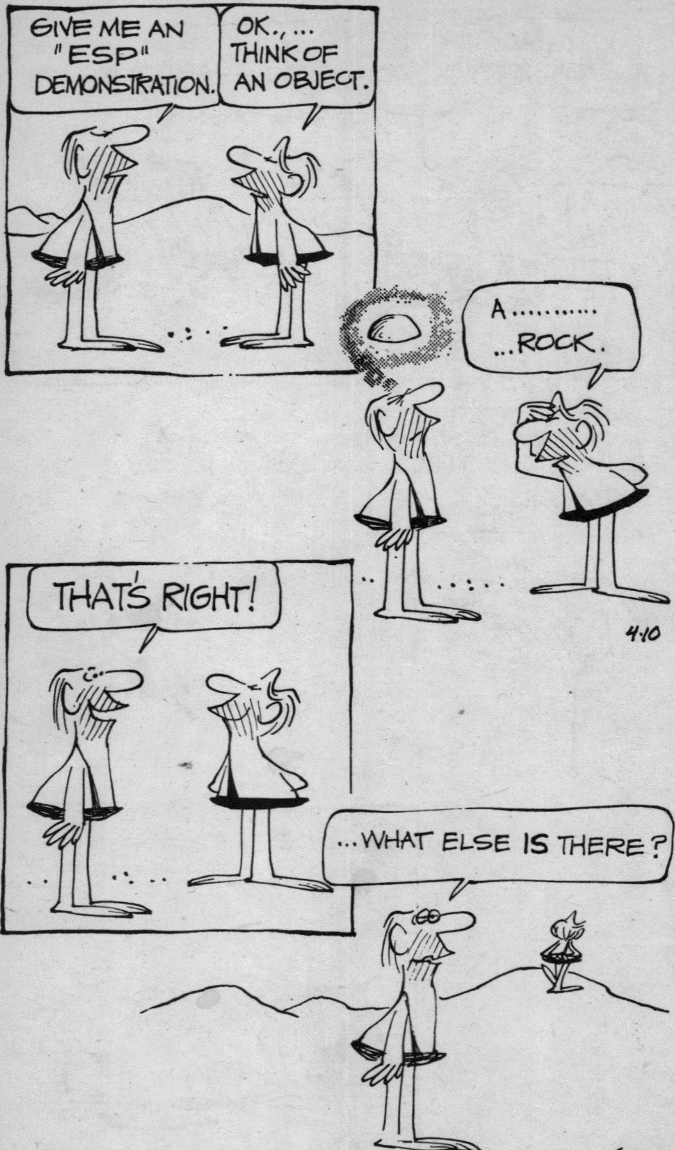

GIVE ME AN "ESP" DEMONSTRATION.
OK., ... THINK OF AN OBJECT.
A..........
...ROCK.
THAT'S RIGHT!
...WHAT ELSE IS THERE?
4·10
hart

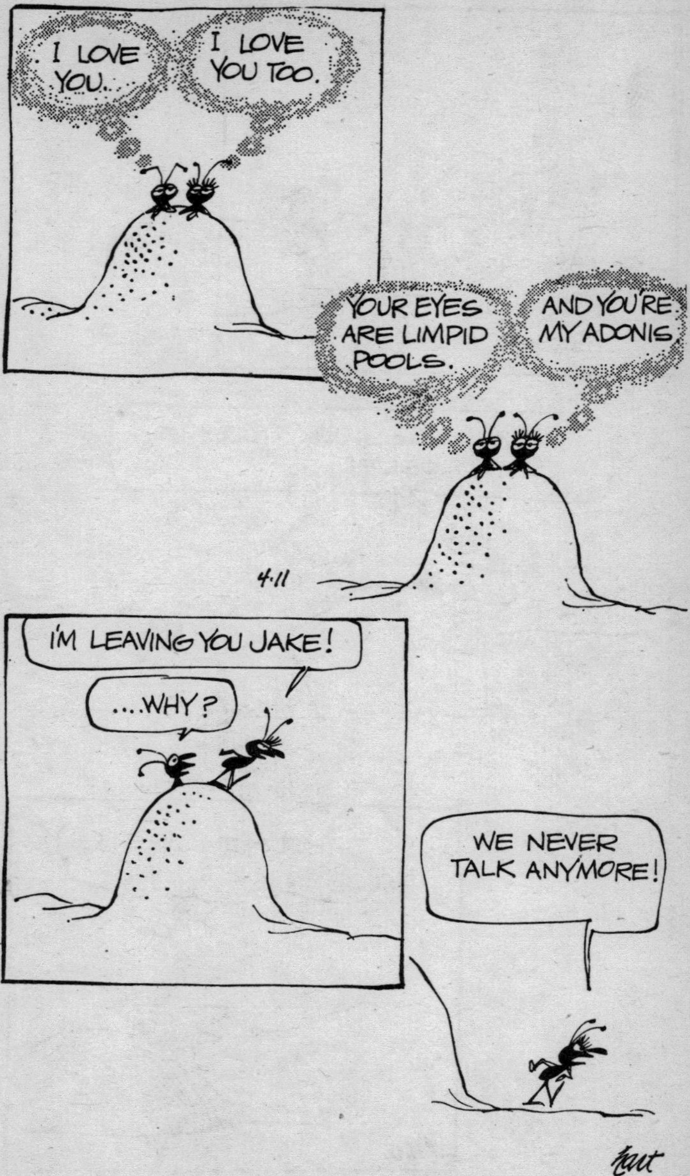
I LOVE YOU...
I LOVE YOU TOO.
YOUR EYES ARE LIMPID POOLS.
AND YOU'RE MY ADONIS
4·11
I'M LEAVING YOU JAKE!
....WHY?
WE NEVER TALK ANYMORE!
hart

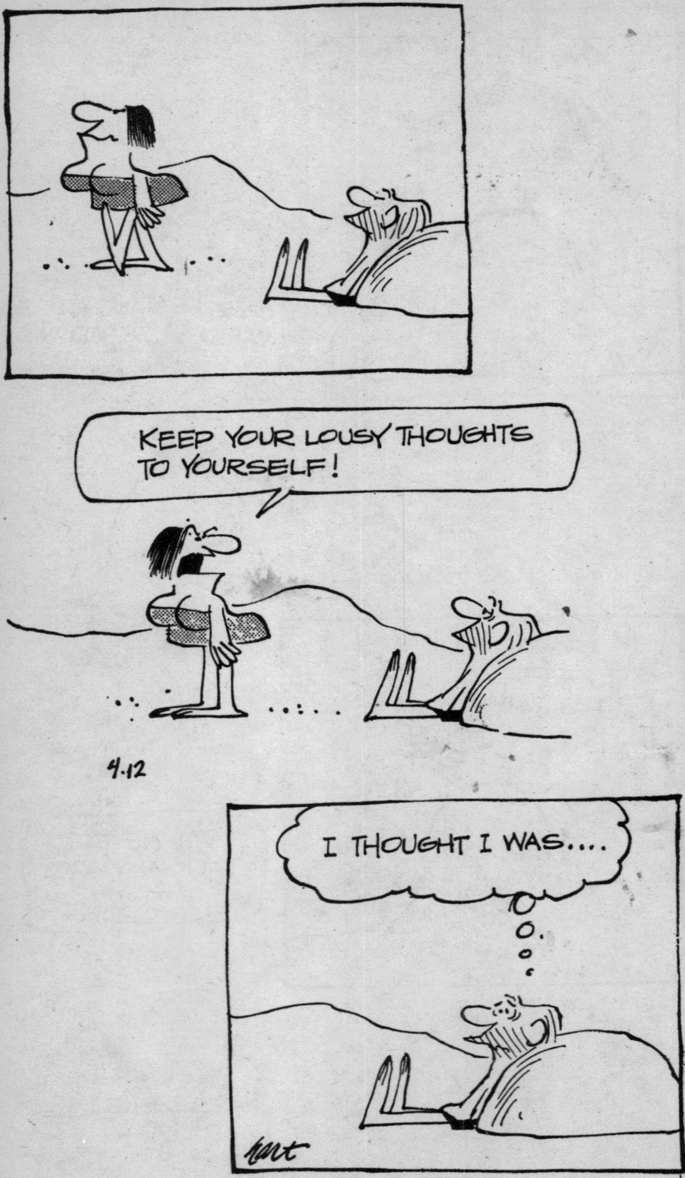
KEEP YOUR LOUSY THOUGHTS TO YOURSELF!
I THOUGHT I WAS....

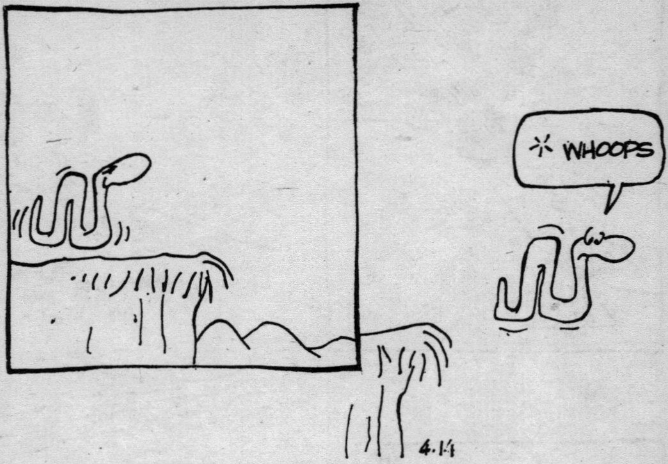

* WHOOPS
4.14

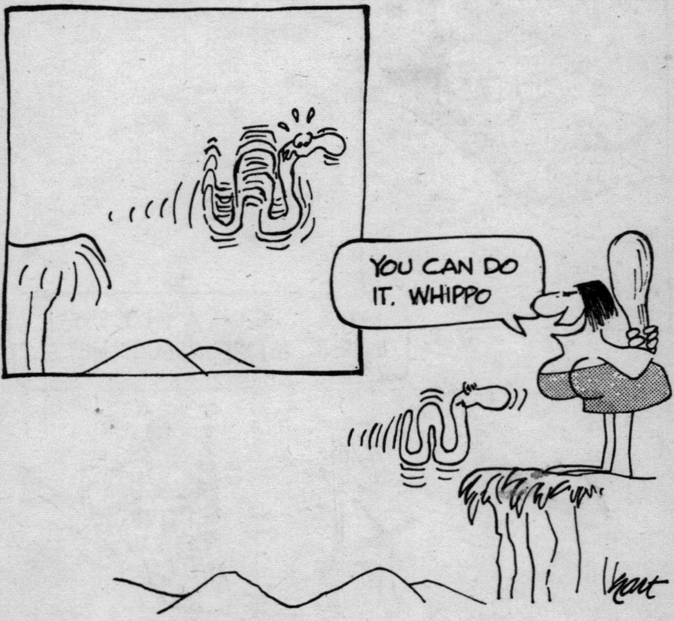

YOU CAN DO IT, WHIPPO

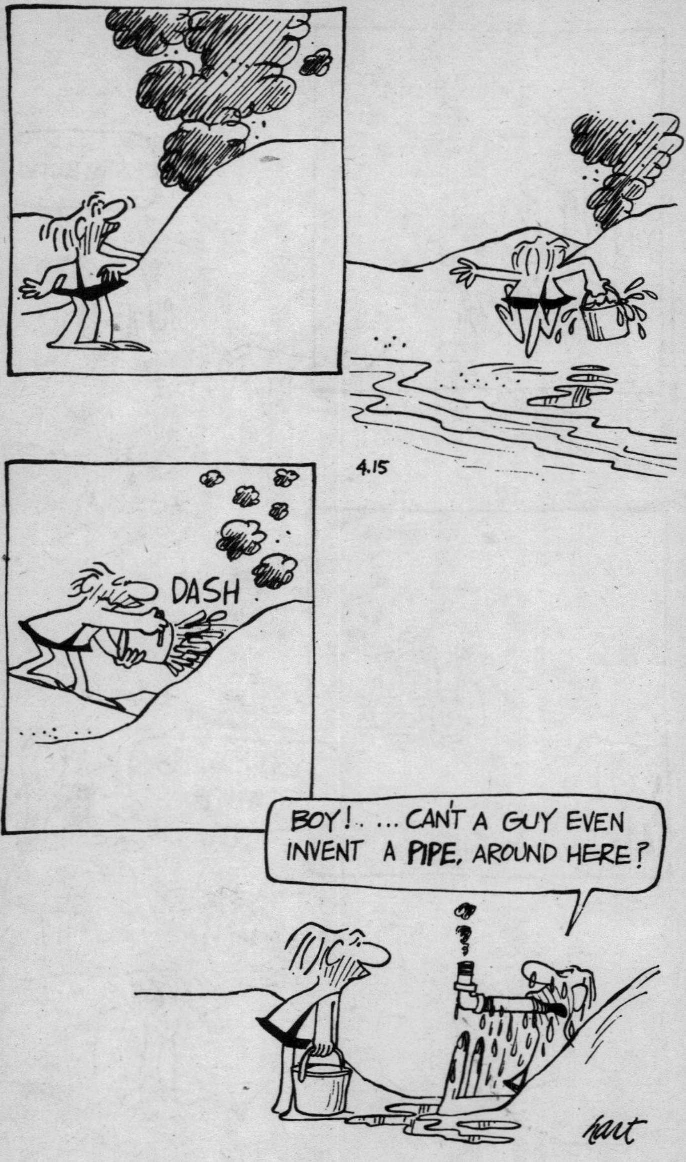
DASH
4.15
BOY!.. ...CAN'T A GUY EVEN INVENT A PIPE, AROUND HERE?
hart

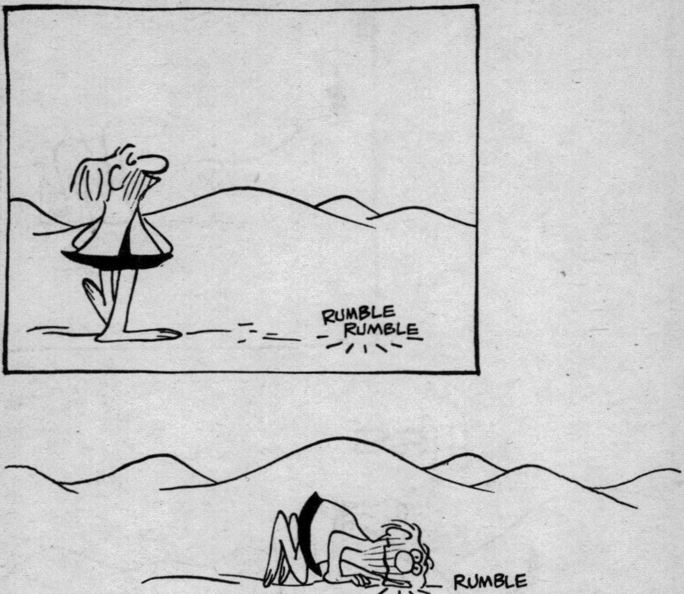
RUMBLE
RUMBLE
RUMBLE

4.16

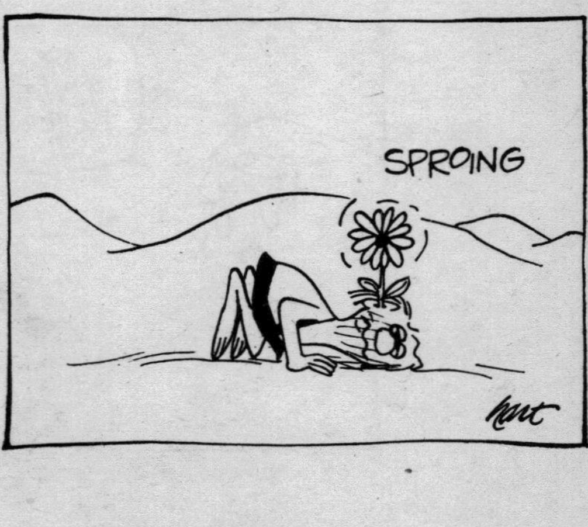
SPROING

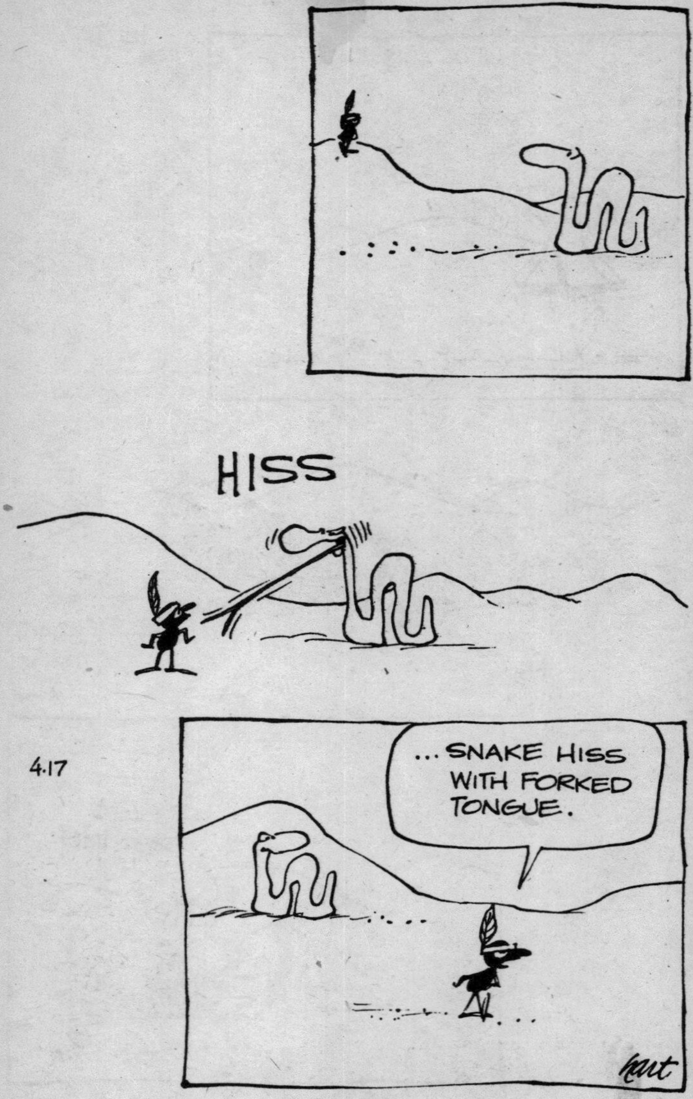
HISS
... SNAKE HISS WITH FORKED TONGUE.
4.17
hart

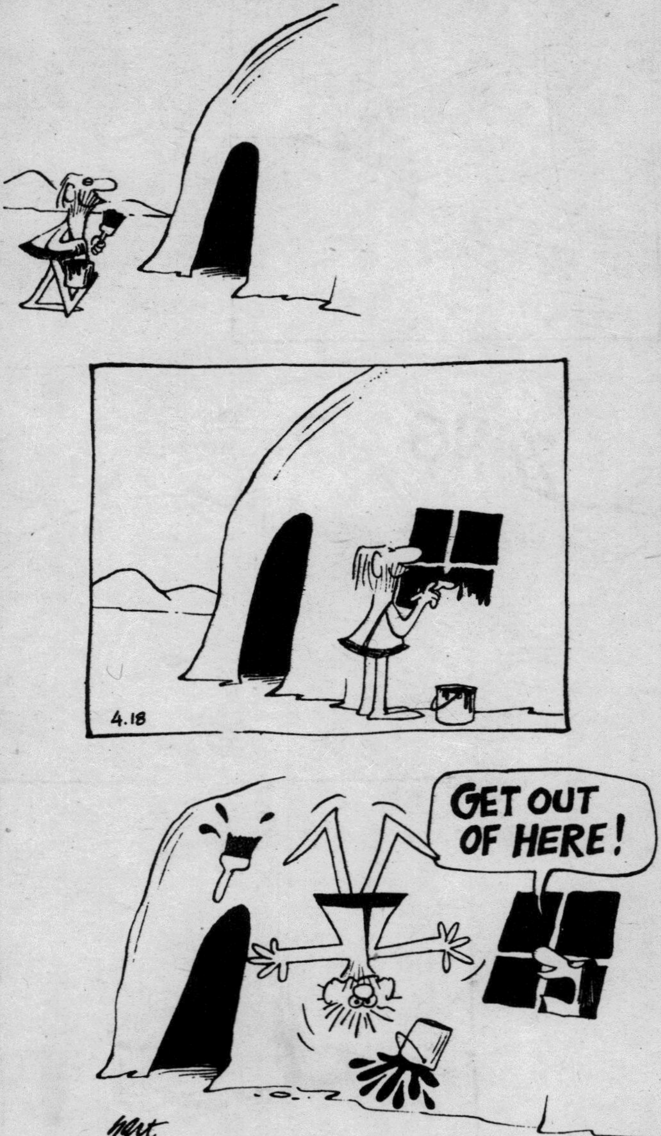
4.18
GET OUT OF HERE!
hart

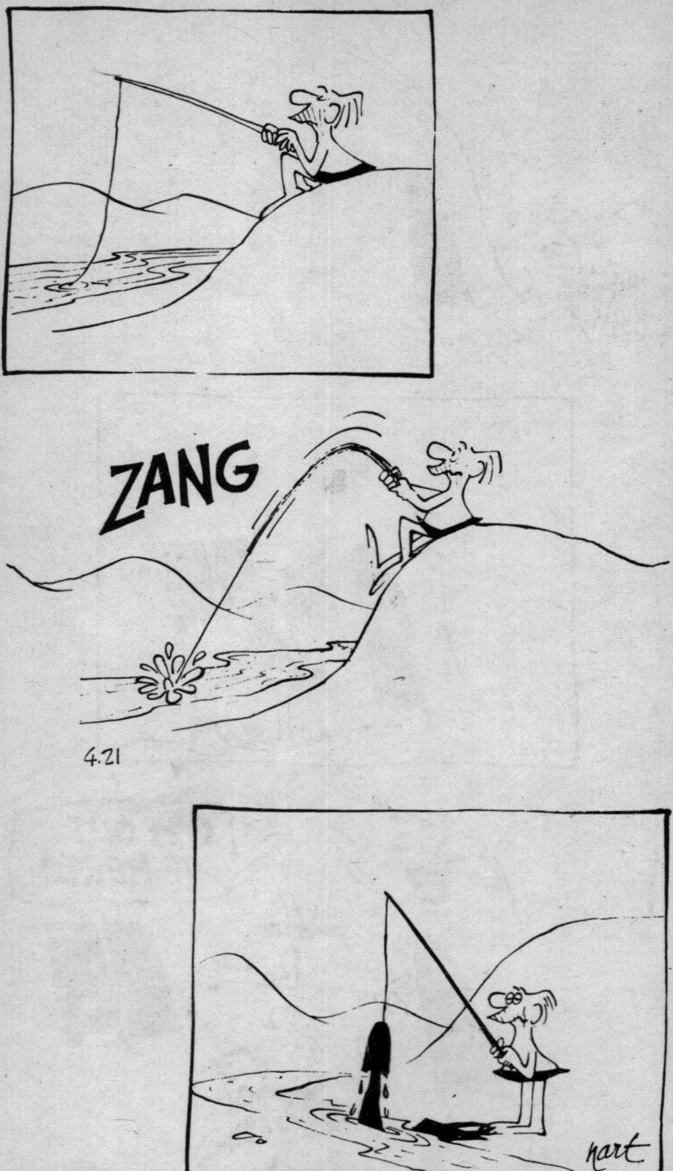
ZANG
4.21
hart

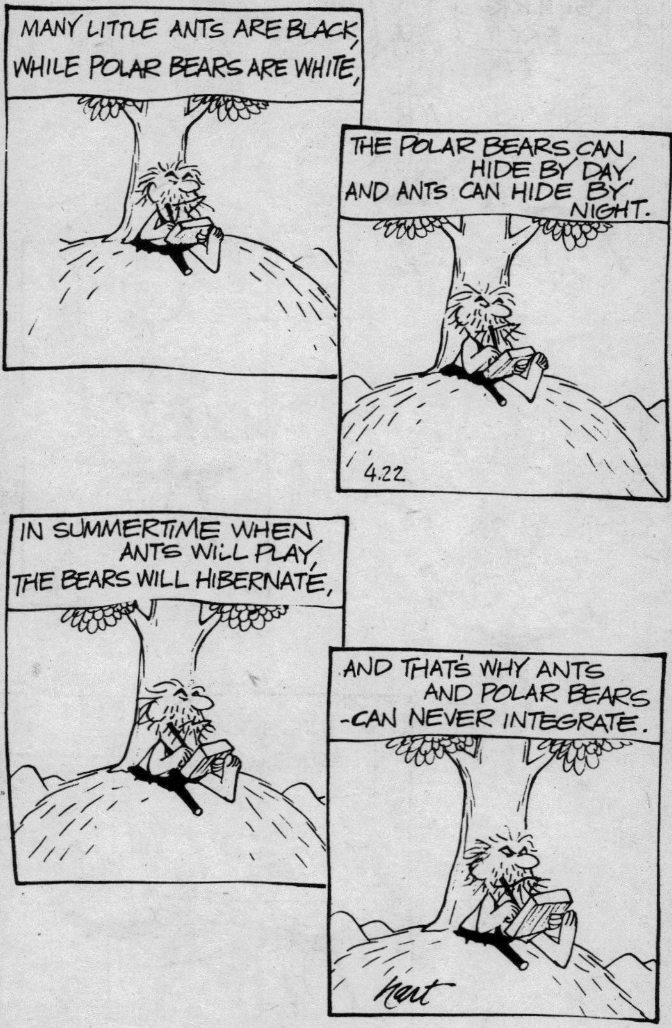

MANY LITTLE ANTS ARE BLACK,
WHILE POLAR BEARS ARE WHITE,
THE POLAR BEARS CAN HIDE BY DAY,
AND ANTS CAN HIDE BY NIGHT.
4.22
IN SUMMERTIME WHEN ANTS WILL PLAY,
THE BEARS WILL HIBERNATE,
AND THAT'S WHY ANTS AND POLAR BEARS
-CAN NEVER INTEGRATE.
Kent

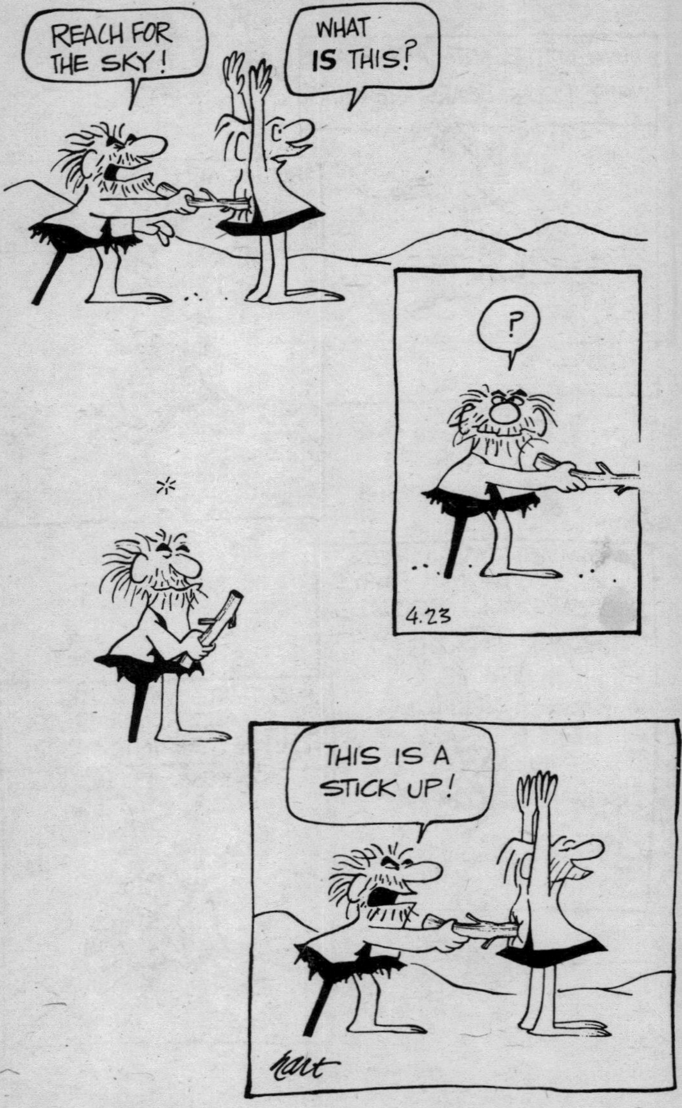
REACH FOR THE SKY!
WHAT IS THIS?
?
4.23
THIS IS A STICK UP!
hart

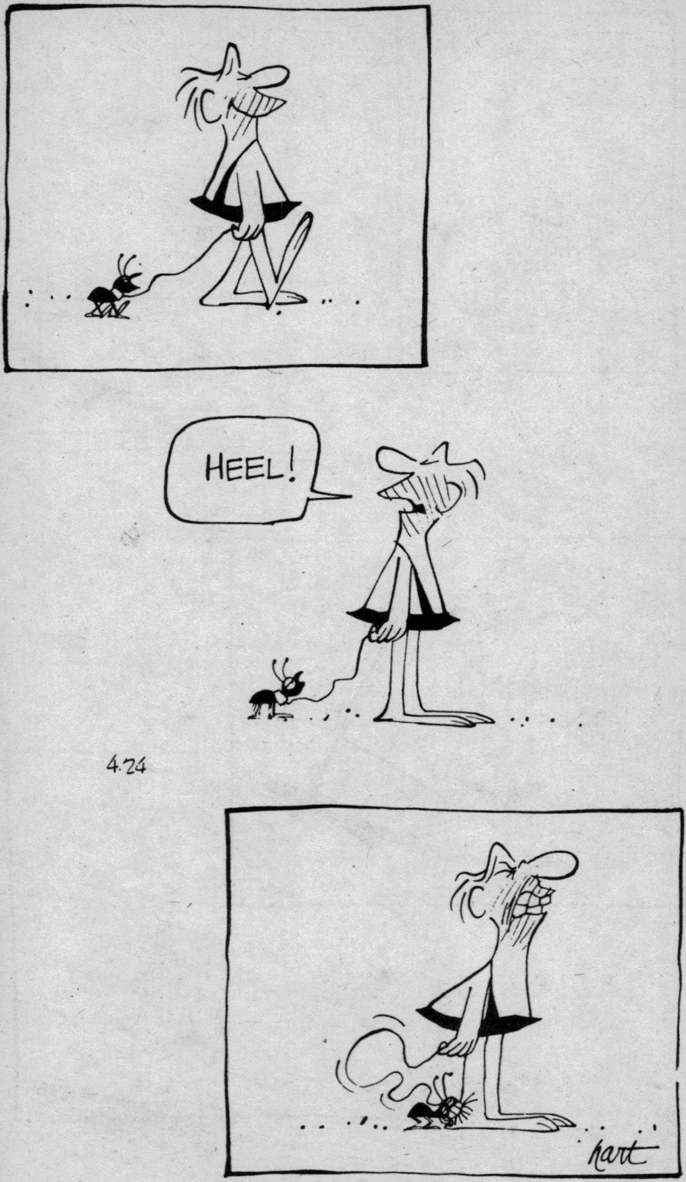
HEEL!
4.24
hart

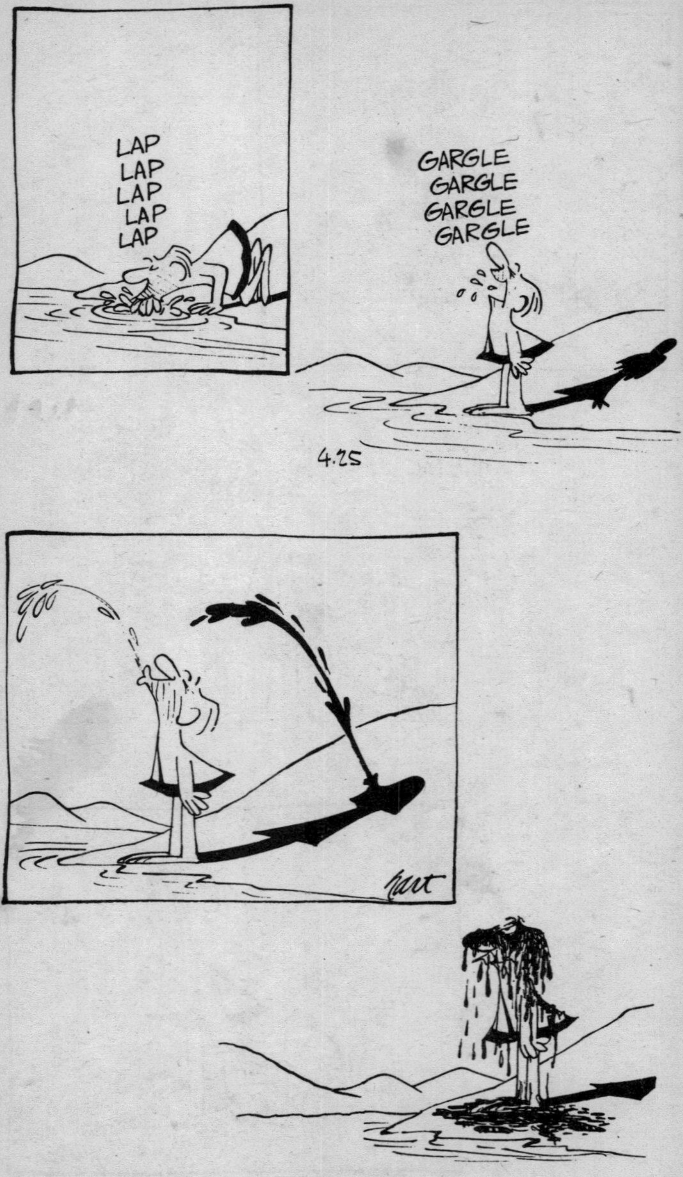
LAP
LAP
LAP
LAP
LAP
GARGLE
GARGLE
GARGLE
GARGLE
4.25
hart

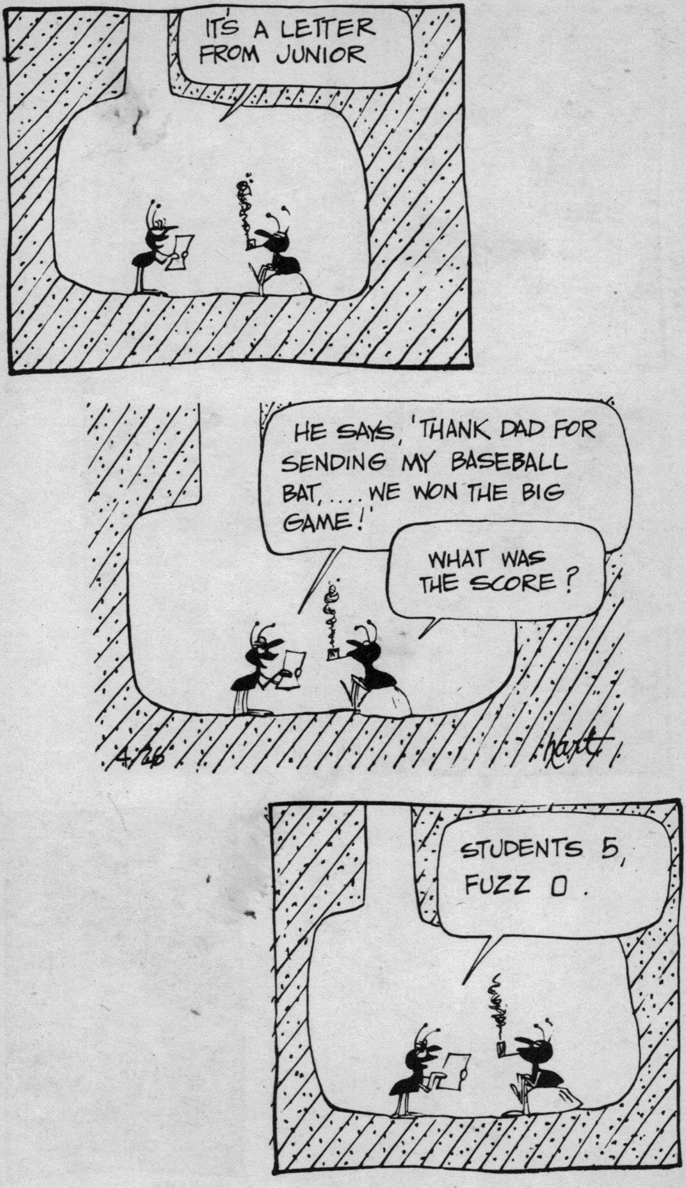
IT'S A LETTER FROM JUNIOR
HE SAYS, 'THANK DAD FOR SENDING MY BASEBALL BAT, ... WE WON THE BIG GAME!'
WHAT WAS THE SCORE?
STUDENTS 5, FUZZ 0.

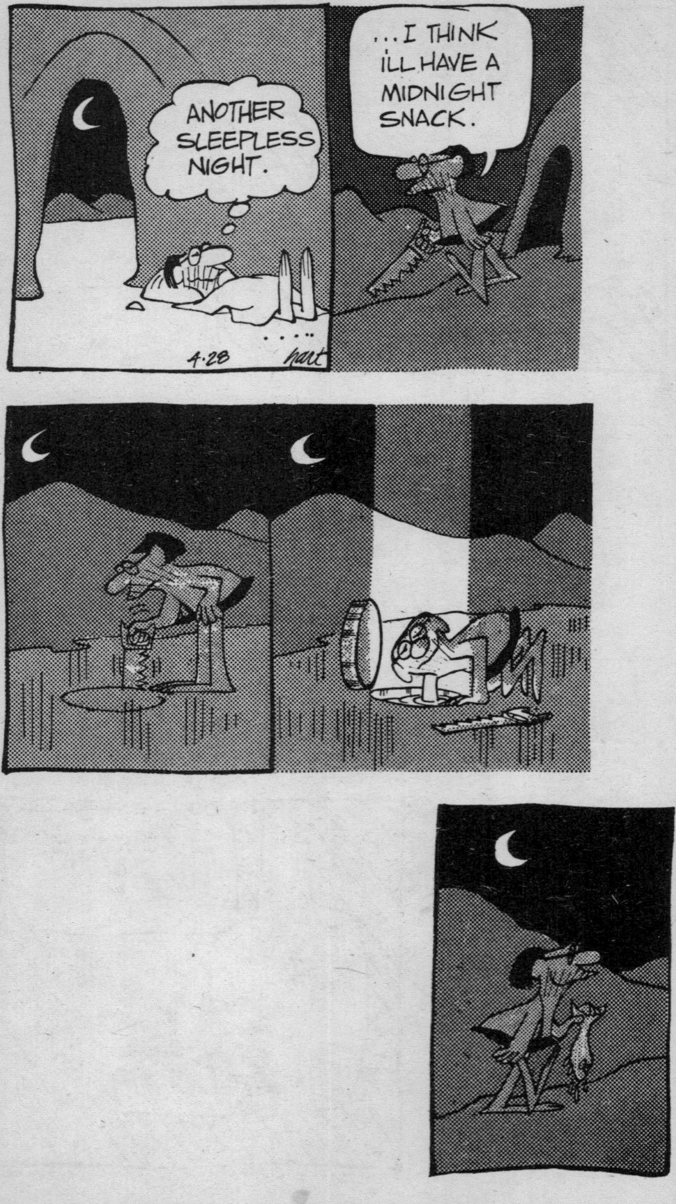
ANOTHER SLEEPLESS NIGHT.
...I THINK I'LL HAVE A MIDNIGHT SNACK.

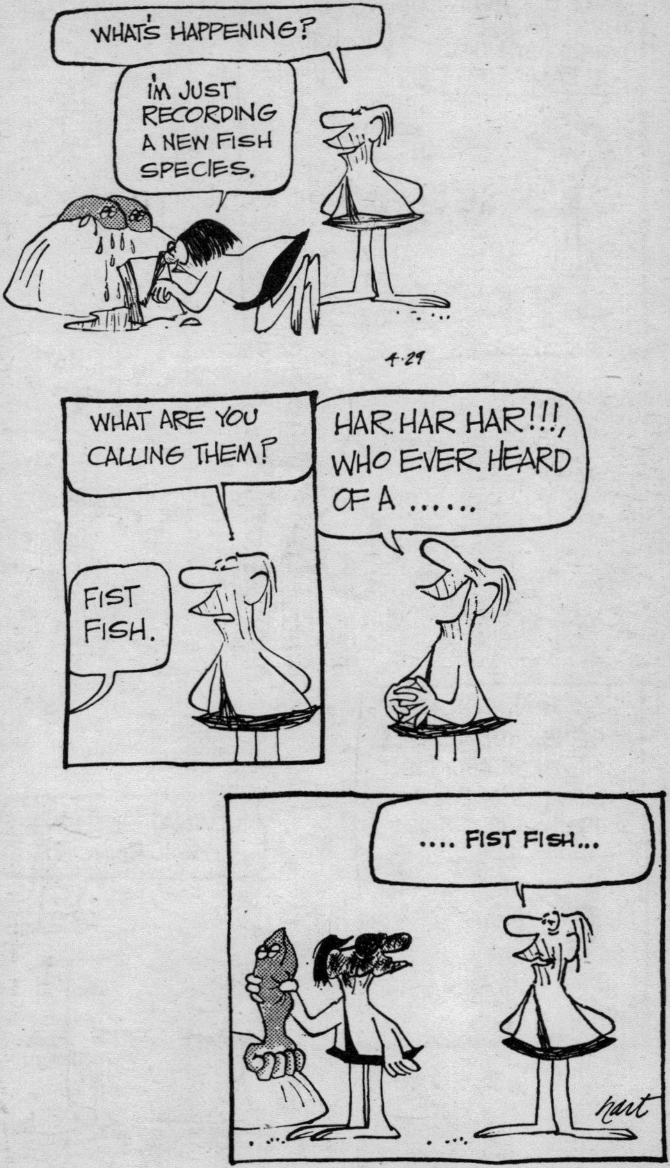
WHAT'S HAPPENING?
I'M JUST RECORDING A NEW FISH SPECIES.
4·29
WHAT ARE YOU CALLING THEM?
FIST FISH.
HAR. HAR HAR!!!, WHO EVER HEARD OF A ......
.... FIST FISH...
hart

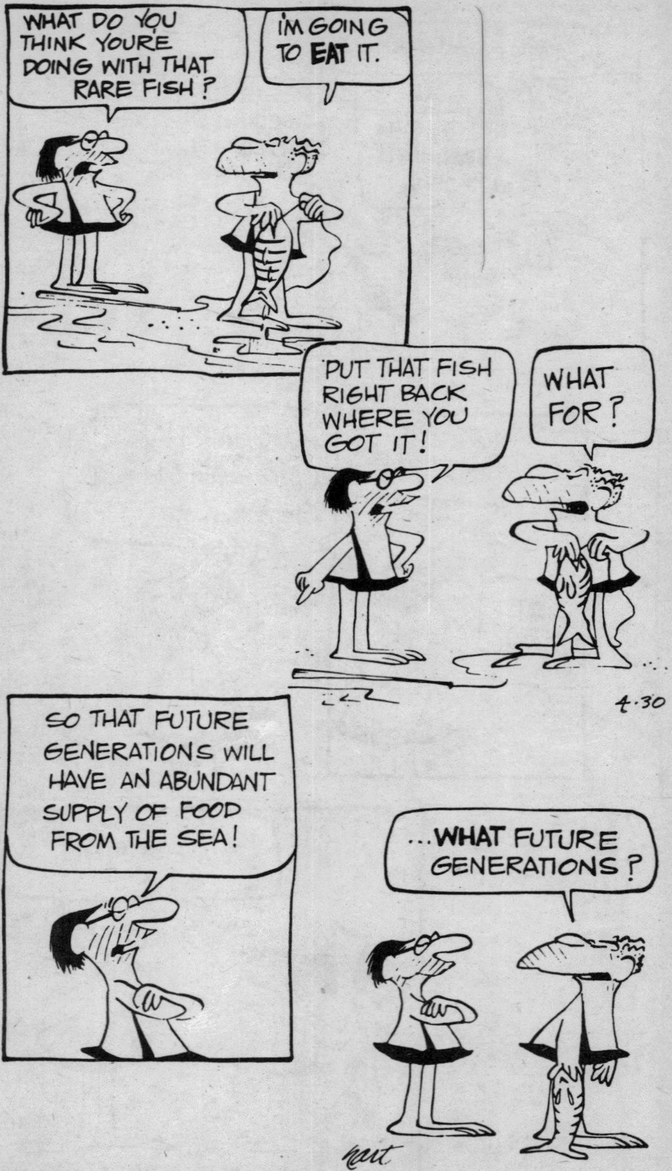
WHAT DO YOU THINK YOU'RE DOING WITH THAT RARE FISH?
I'M GOING TO **EAT** IT.
PUT THAT FISH RIGHT BACK WHERE YOU GOT IT!
WHAT FOR?
4·30
SO THAT FUTURE GENERATIONS WILL HAVE AN ABUNDANT SUPPLY OF FOOD FROM THE SEA!
...**WHAT** FUTURE GENERATIONS?
hart

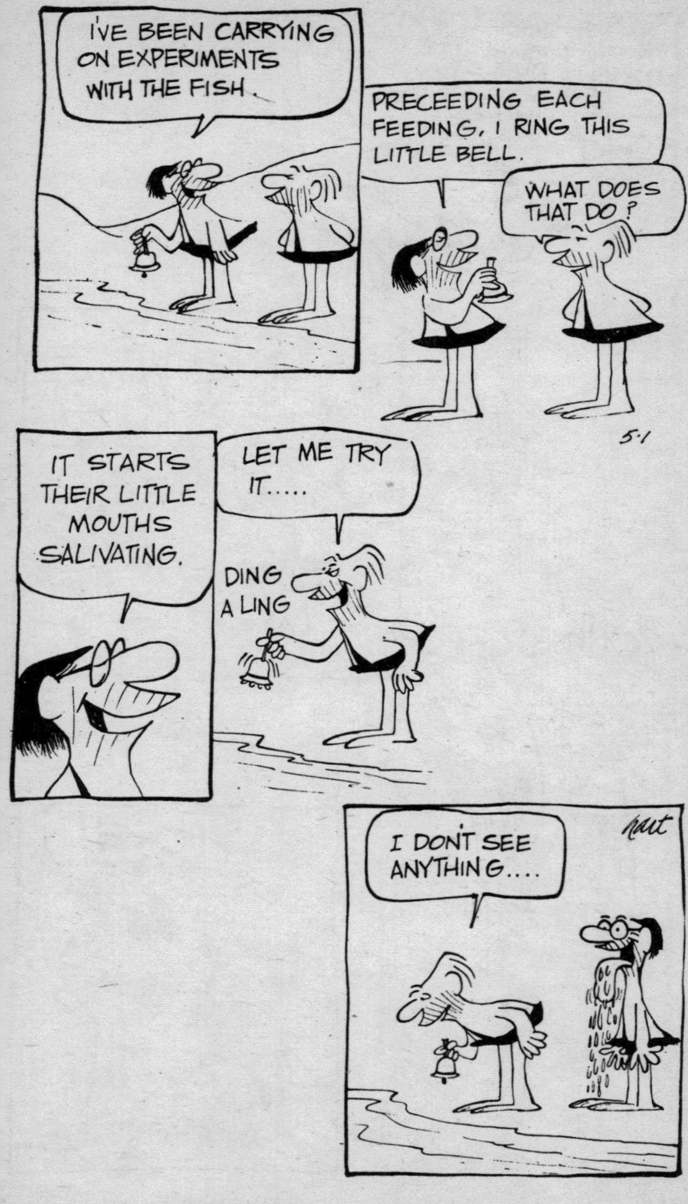
I'VE BEEN CARRYING ON EXPERIMENTS WITH THE FISH.
PRECEEDING EACH FEEDING, I RING THIS LITTLE BELL.
WHAT DOES THAT DO ?
5·1
IT STARTS THEIR LITTLE MOUTHS SALIVATING.
LET ME TRY IT.....
DING A LING
I DON'T SEE ANYTHING....
hart

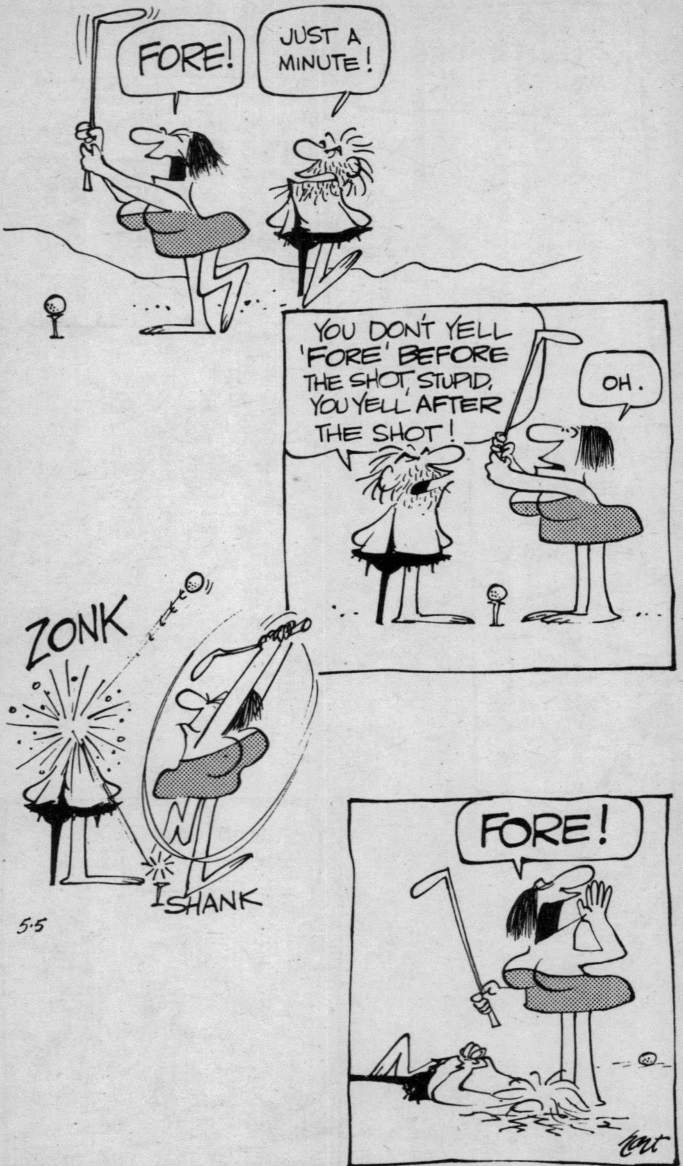
FORE!
JUST A MINUTE!
YOU DON'T YELL 'FORE' BEFORE THE SHOT, STUPID, YOU YELL AFTER THE SHOT!
OH.
ZONK
SHANK
5·5
FORE!

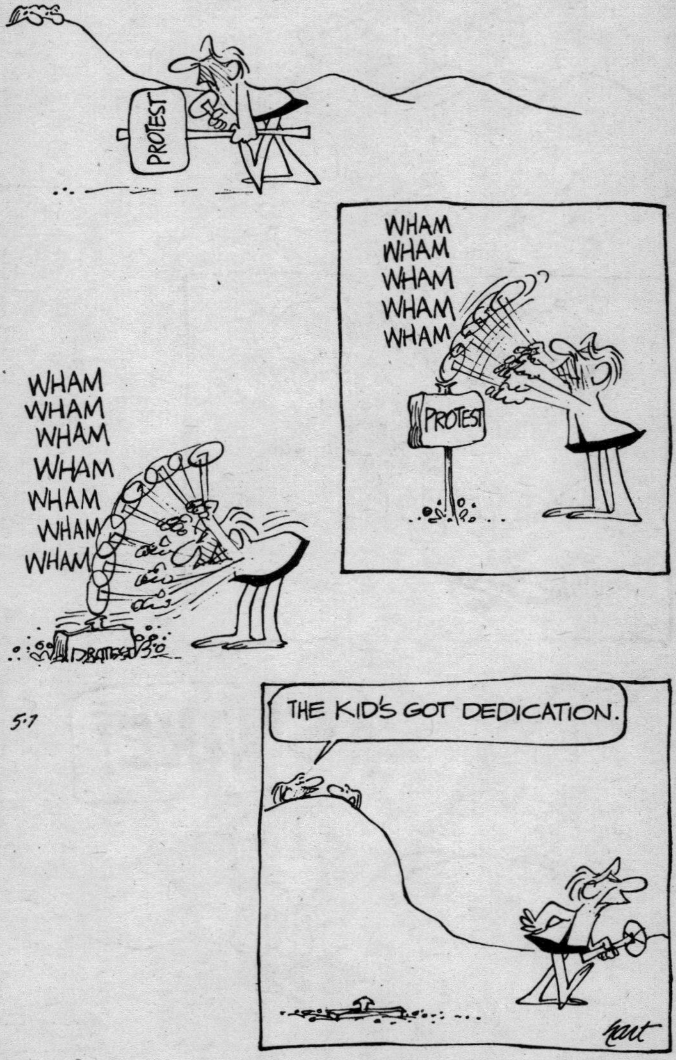
PROTEST
WHAM
WHAM
WHAM
WHAM
WHAM
PROTEST
WHAM
WHAM
WHAM
WHAM
WHAM
WHAM
WHAM
5·7
THE KID'S GOT DEDICATION.
hart

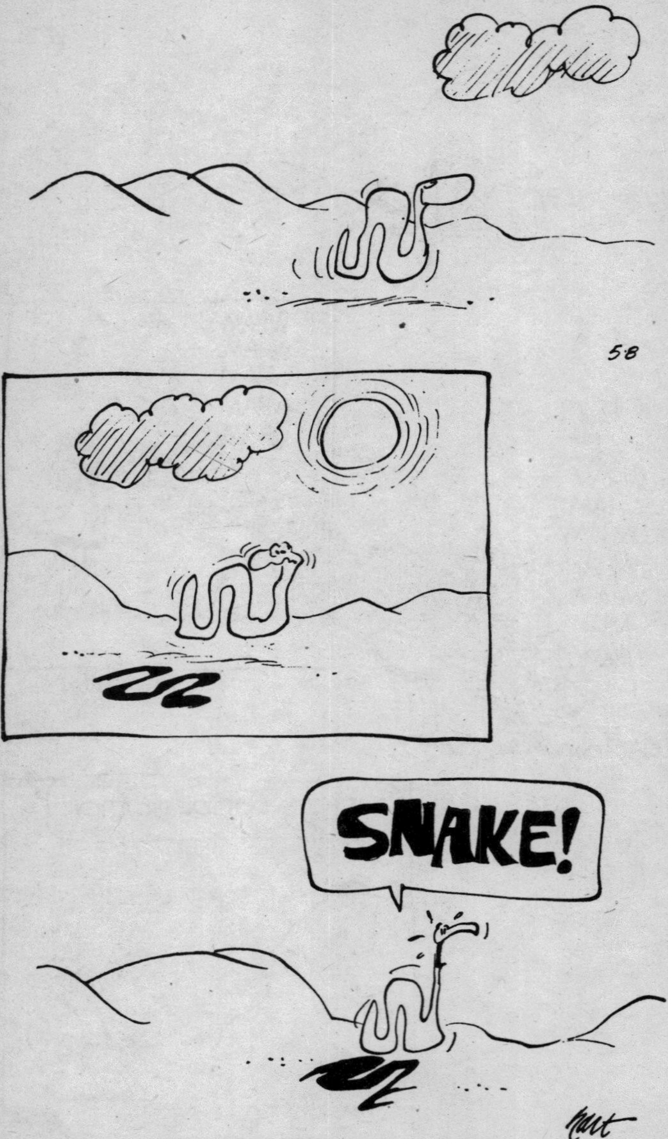
5·8
SNAKE!
hart

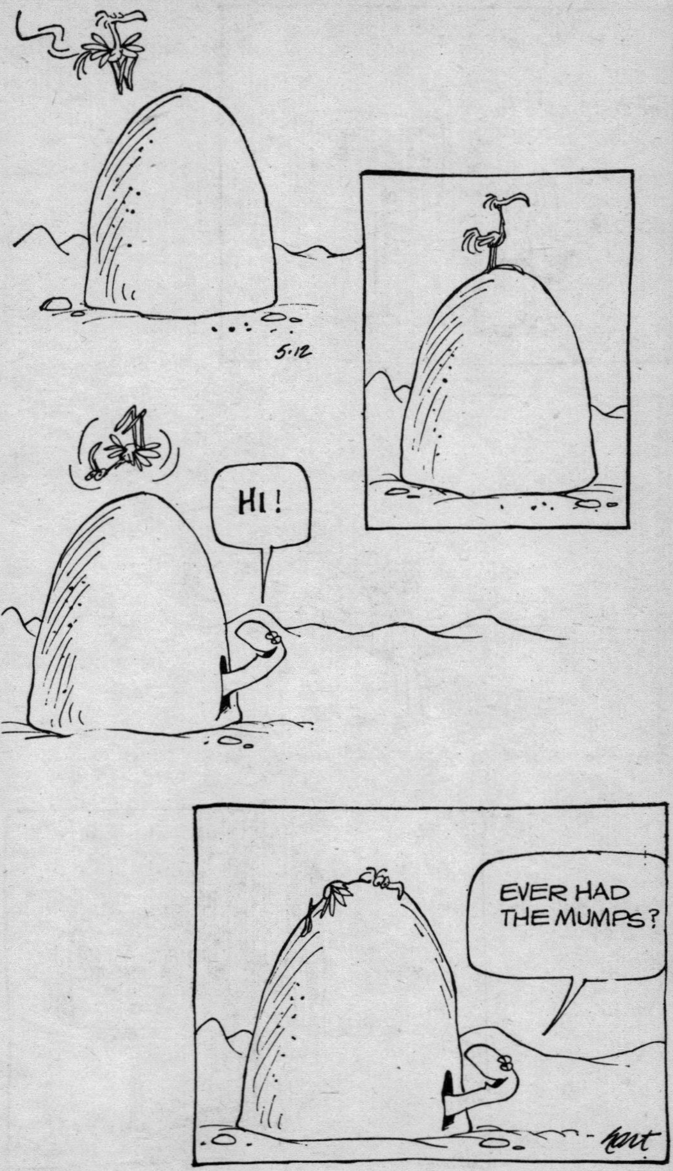
5·12
HI!
EVER HAD THE MUMPS?
hart

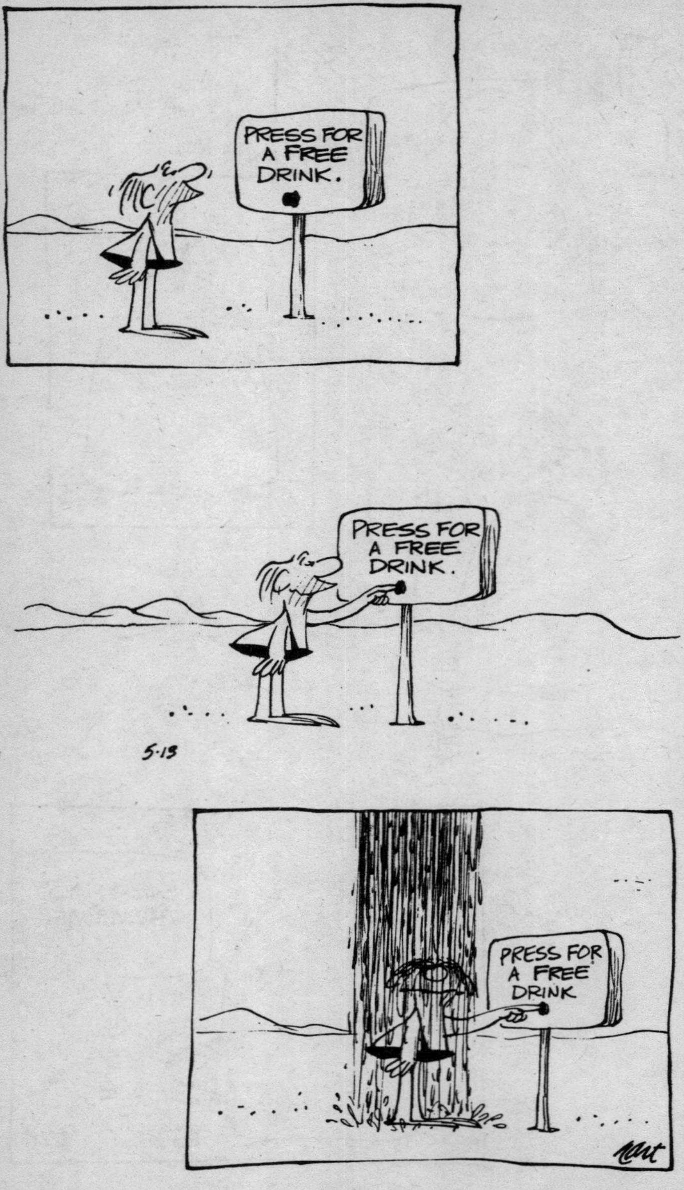
PRESS FOR A FREE DRINK.
PRESS FOR A FREE DRINK.
5-13
PRESS FOR A FREE DRINK

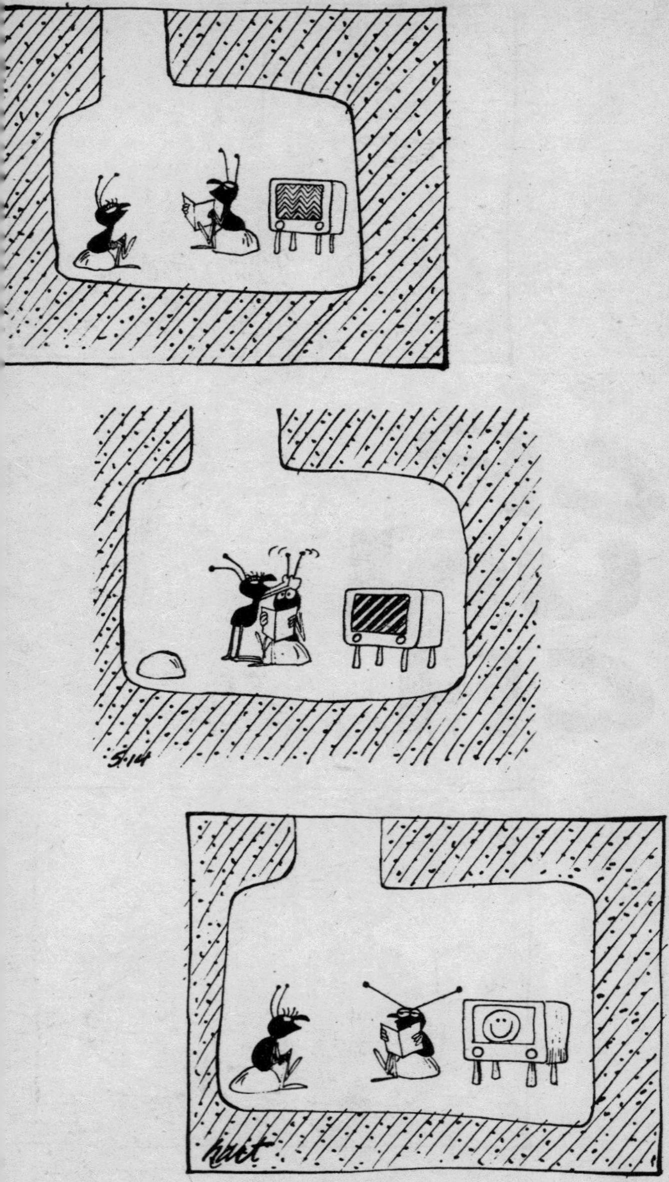
5-14
hart

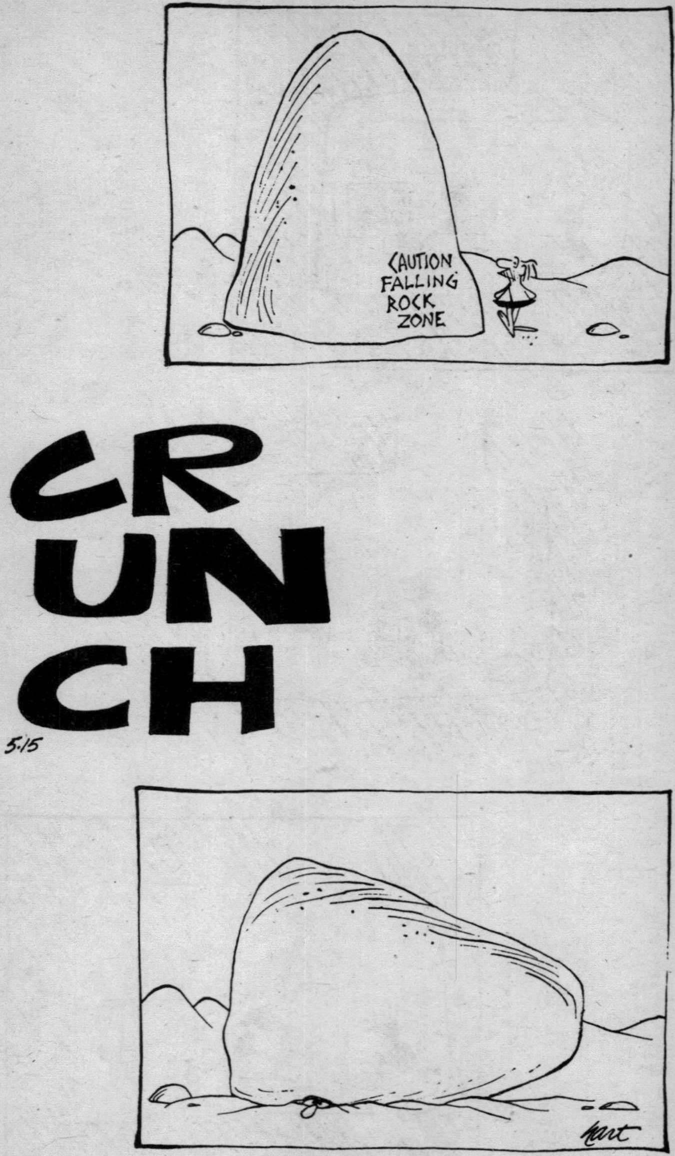
CAUTION
FALLING
ROCK
ZONE
CRUNCH
5·15
hart

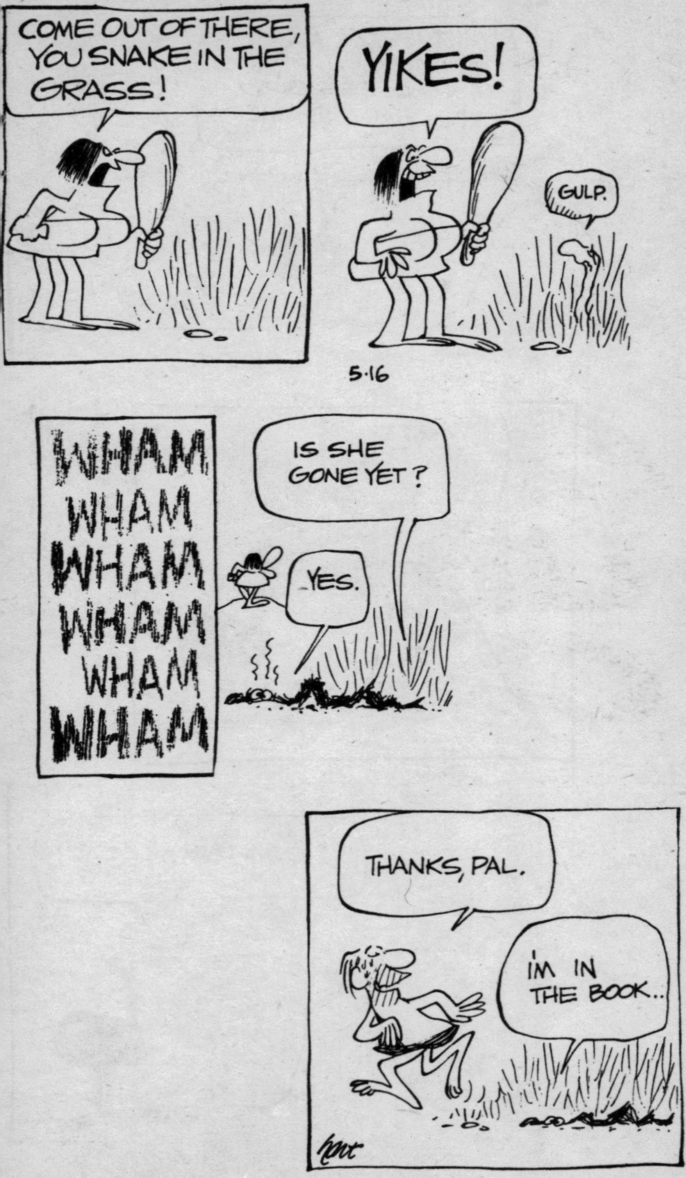
COME OUT OF THERE, YOU SNAKE IN THE GRASS!
YIKES!
GULP.
5·16
WHAM WHAM WHAM WHAM WHAM WHAM
IS SHE GONE YET?
YES.
THANKS, PAL.
I'M IN THE BOOK..
hart

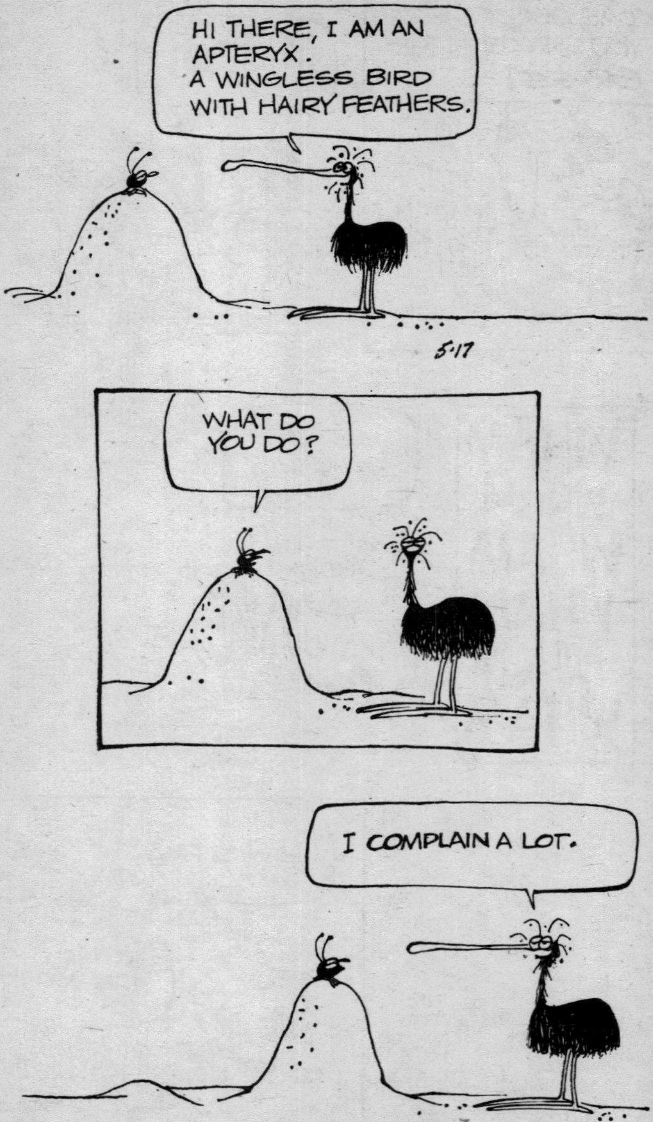
HI THERE, I AM AN APTERYX. A WINGLESS BIRD WITH HAIRY FEATHERS.
5·17
WHAT DO YOU DO?
I COMPLAIN A LOT.

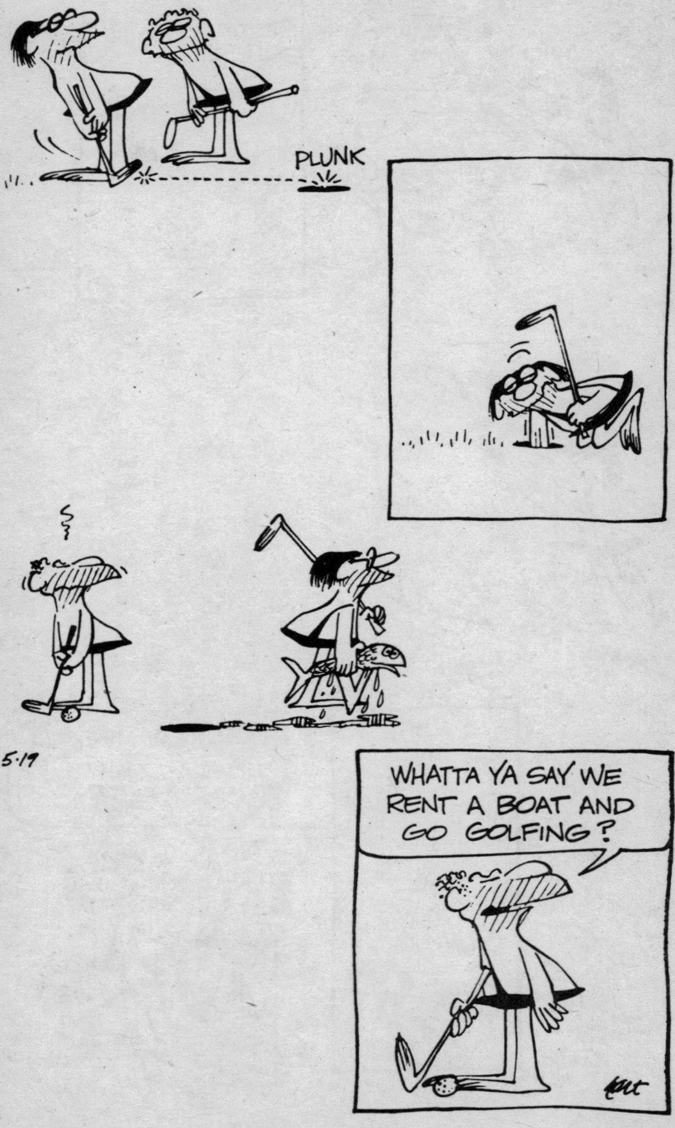
PLUNK
5·19
WHATTA YA SAY WE RENT A BOAT AND GO GOLFING?

ZAK
CHUNK
ZAK
5·20
CHUNK
I JUST REMEMBERED, I HAVE A DENTAL APPOINTMENT.

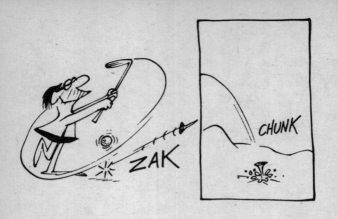

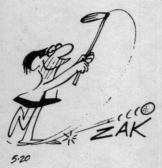

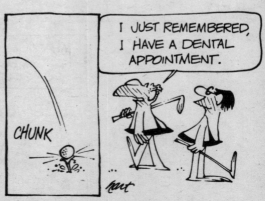

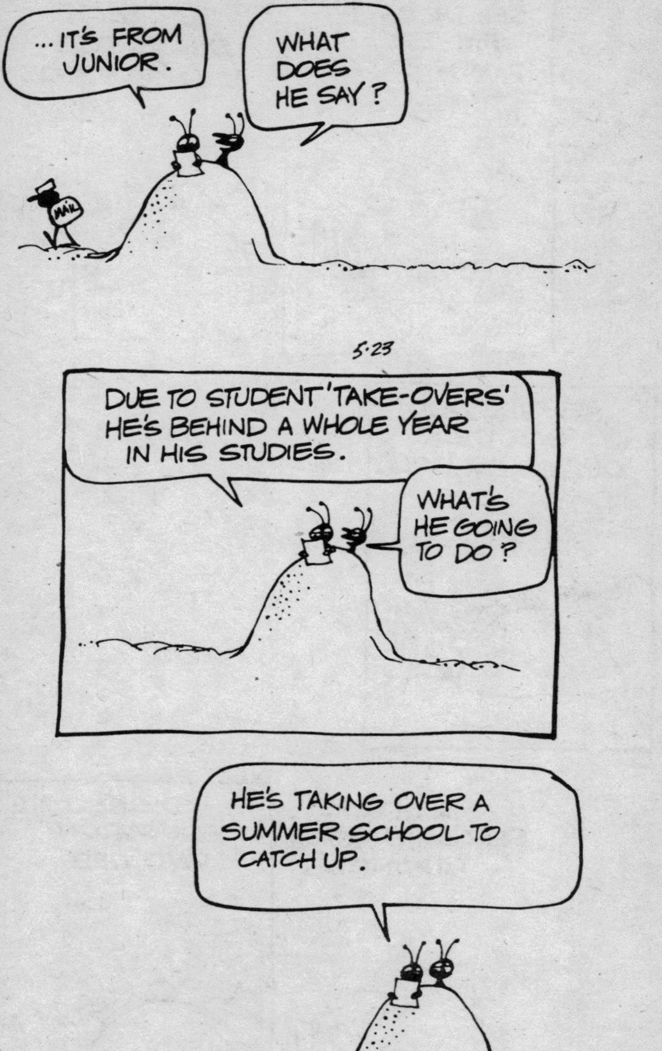

... IT'S FROM JUNIOR.
WHAT DOES HE SAY?
5·23
DUE TO STUDENT 'TAKE-OVERS' HE'S BEHIND A WHOLE YEAR IN HIS STUDIES.
WHAT'S HE GOING TO DO?
HE'S TAKING OVER A SUMMER SCHOOL TO CATCH UP.

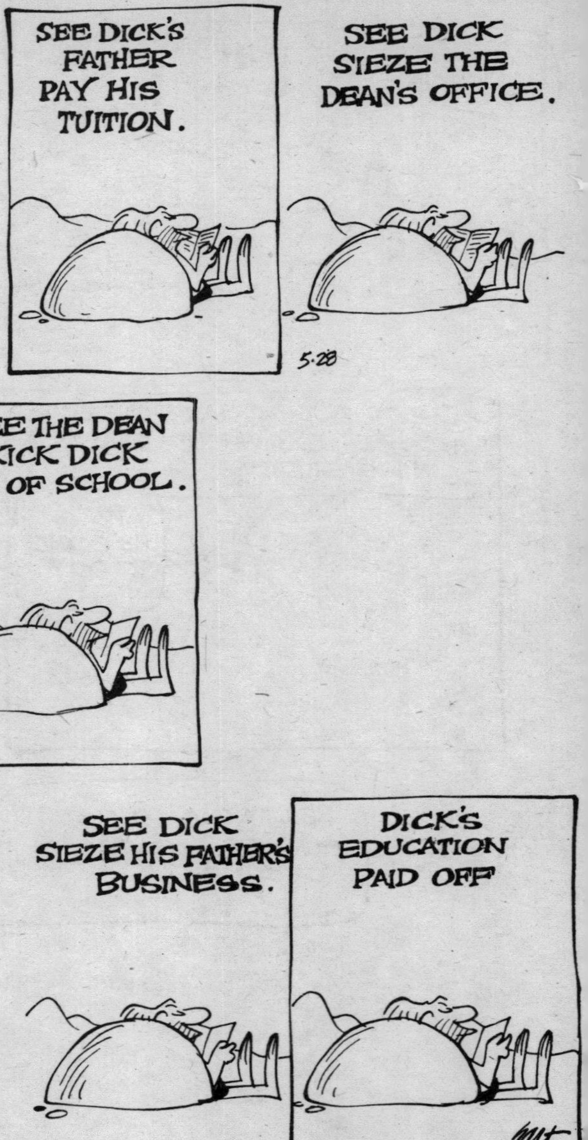
SEE DICK'S FATHER PAY HIS TUITION.
SEE DICK SIEZE THE DEAN'S OFFICE.
5·28
SEE THE DEAN KICK DICK OUT OF SCHOOL.
SEE DICK SIEZE HIS FATHER'S BUSINESS.
DICK'S EDUCATION PAID OFF

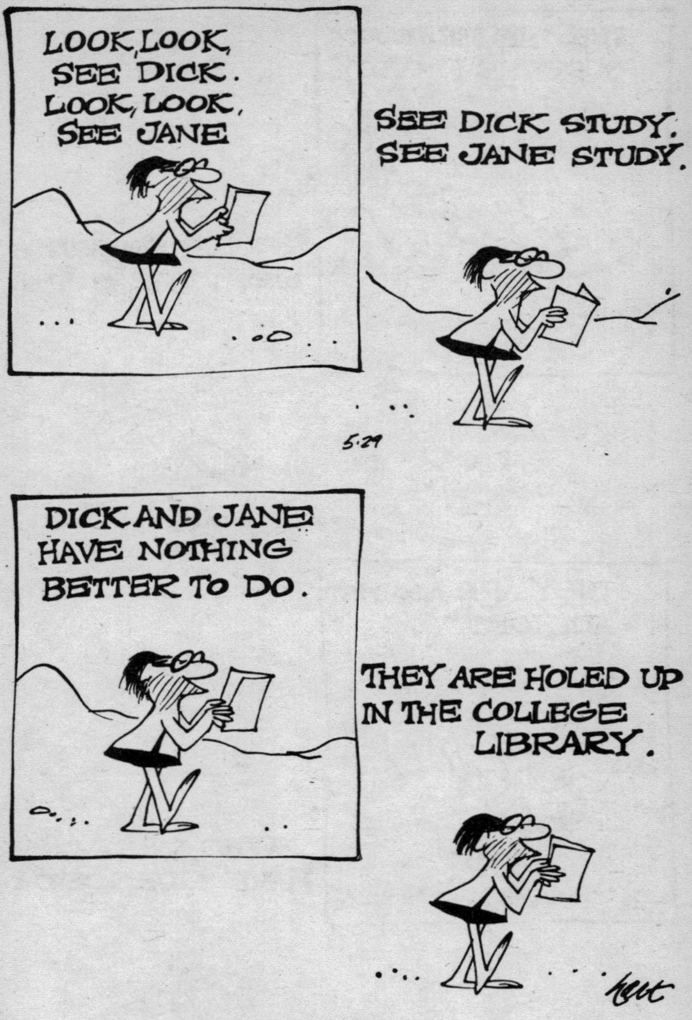
LOOK, LOOK,
SEE DICK.
LOOK, LOOK,
SEE JANE
SEE DICK STUDY.
SEE JANE STUDY.
5·29
DICK AND JANE
HAVE NOTHING
BETTER TO DO.
THEY ARE HOLED UP
IN THE COLLEGE
LIBRARY.
kent

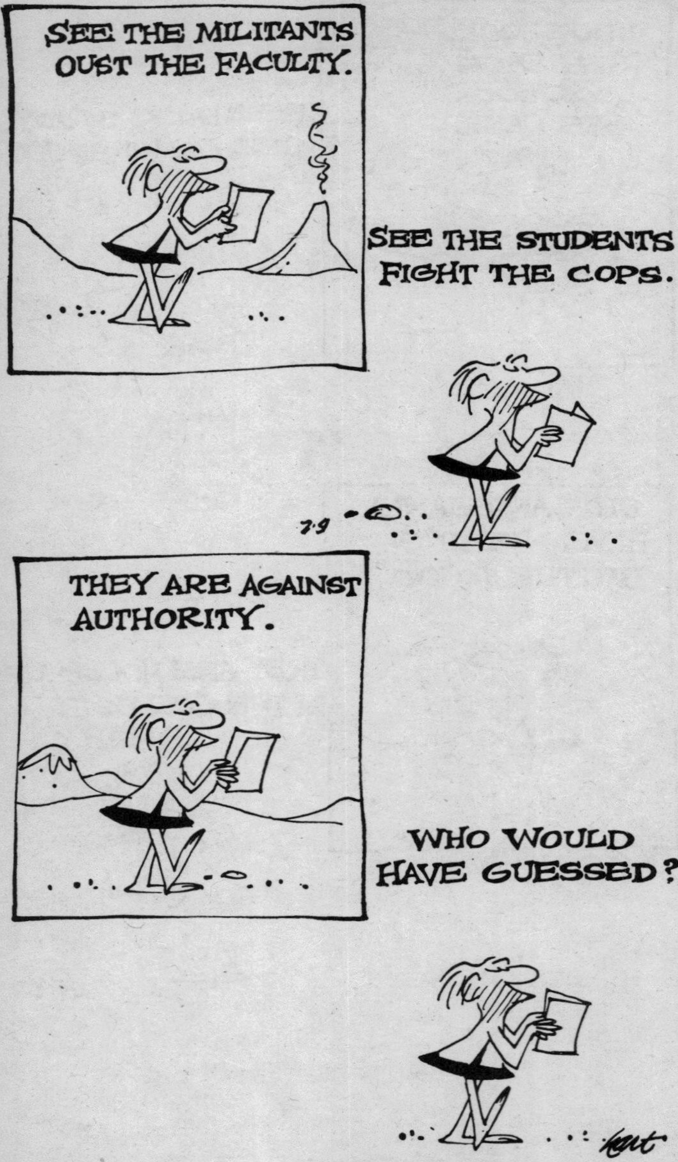

SEE THE MILITANTS OUST THE FACULTY.
SEE THE STUDENTS FIGHT THE COPS.
THEY ARE AGAINST AUTHORITY.
WHO WOULD HAVE GUESSED?

SEE DICK SWEAR
AT THE FACULTY.

SEE DICK SWEAR
AT THE DEAN.

6.3

DICK IS A FOUR LETTER
MAN.

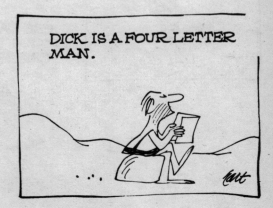

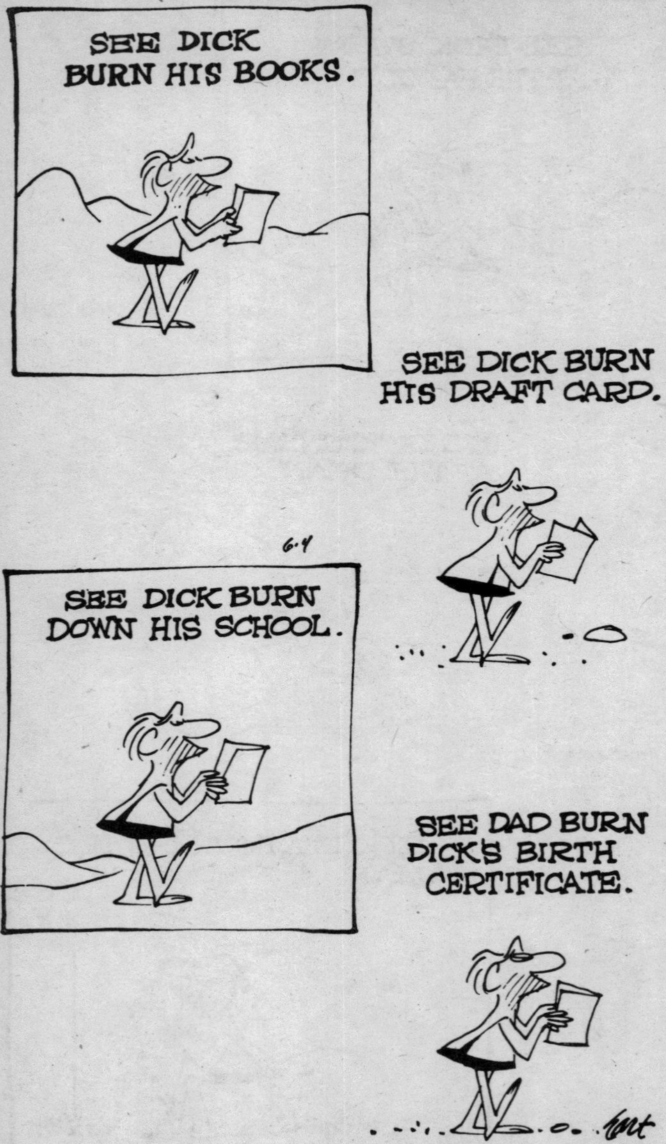
SEE DICK
BURN HIS BOOKS.
SEE DICK BURN
HIS DRAFT CARD.
6·4
SEE DICK BURN
DOWN HIS SCHOOL.
SEE DAD BURN
DICK'S BIRTH
CERTIFICATE.

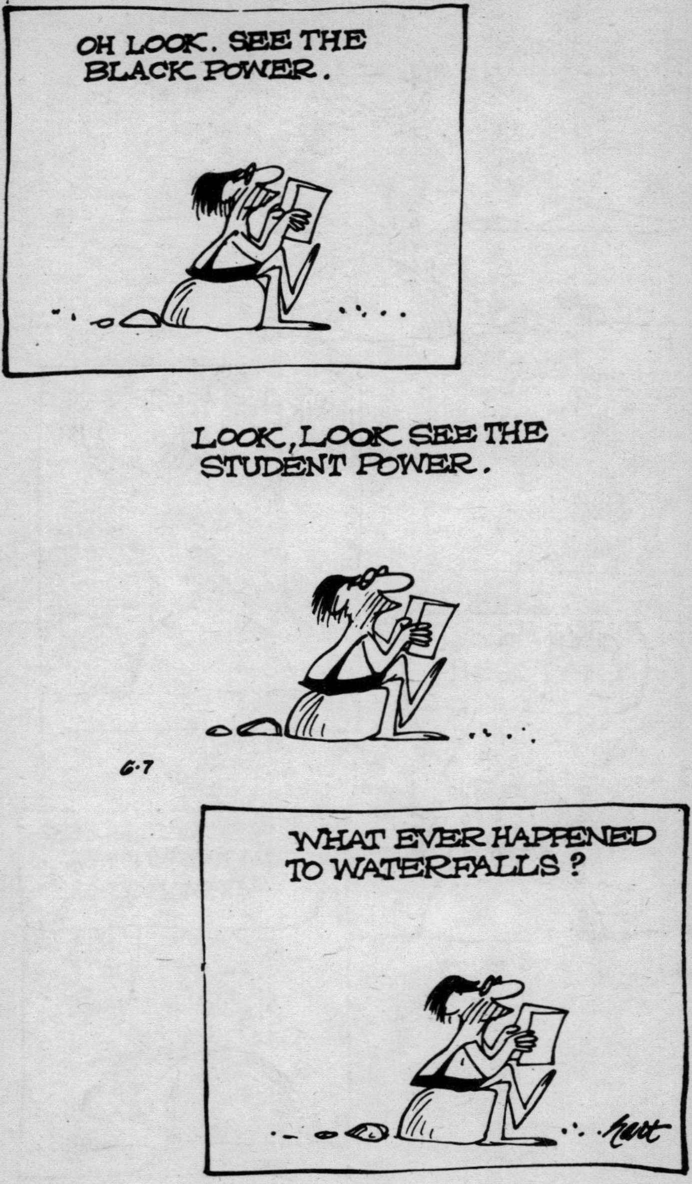
OH LOOK. SEE THE BLACK POWER.
LOOK, LOOK SEE THE STUDENT POWER.
6·7
WHAT EVER HAPPENED TO WATERFALLS?
hart

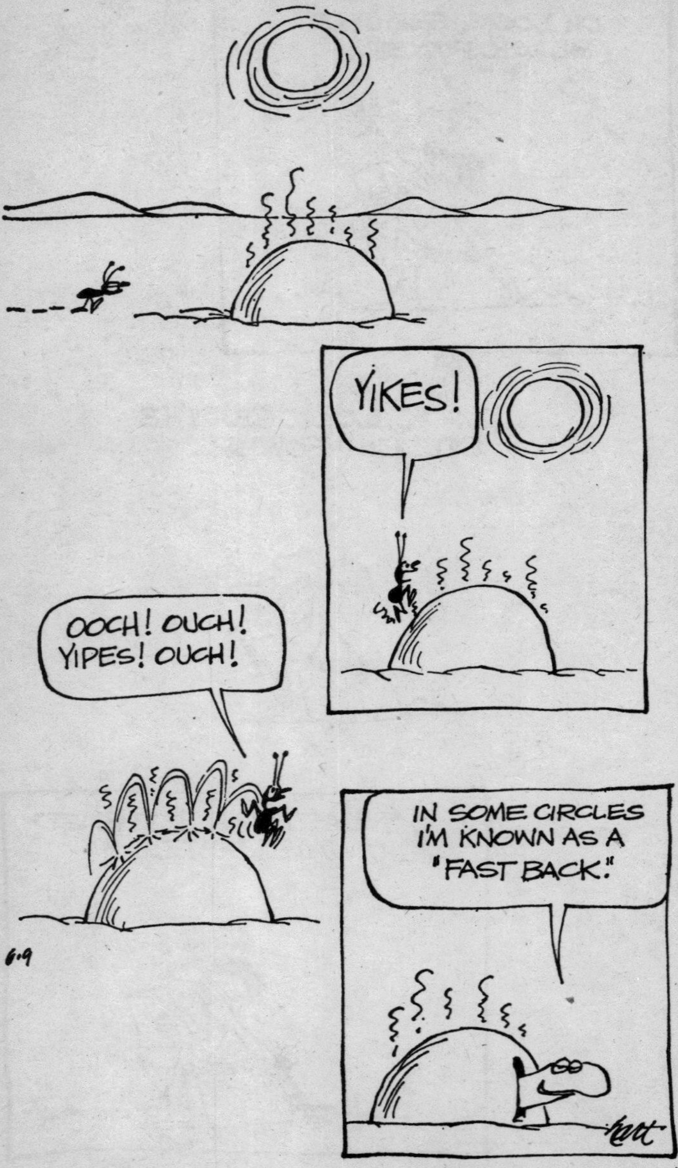
YIKES!
OOCH! OUCH! YIPES! OUCH!
IN SOME CIRCLES I'M KNOWN AS A "FAST BACK."
6-9
hart

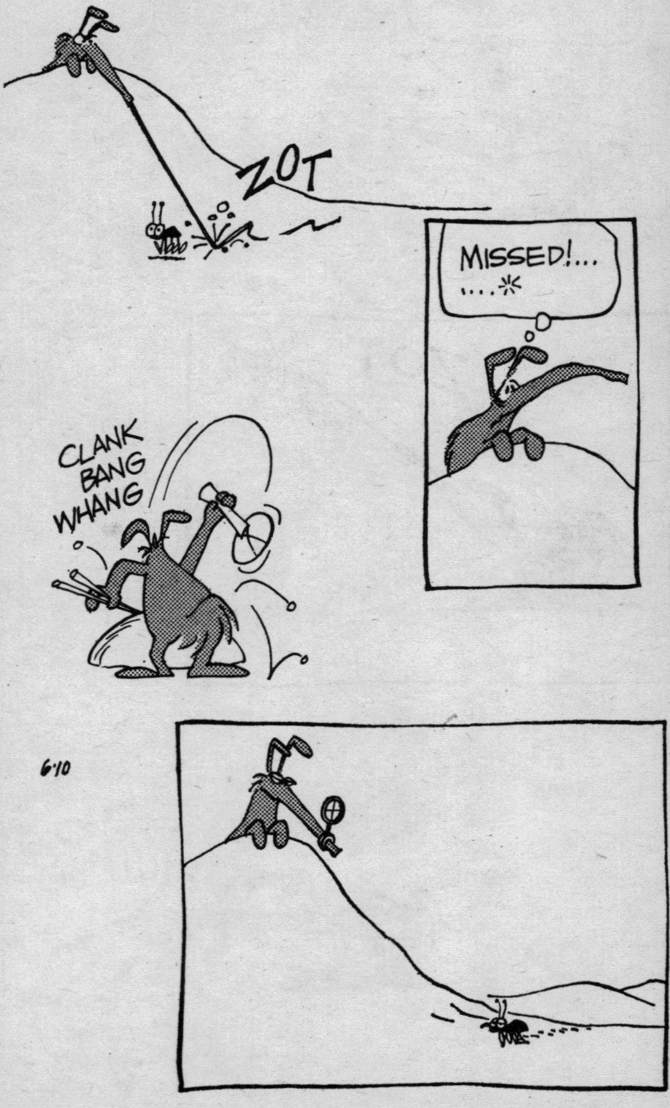
ZOT
MISSED!...
....
CLANK
BANG
WHANG
6·10

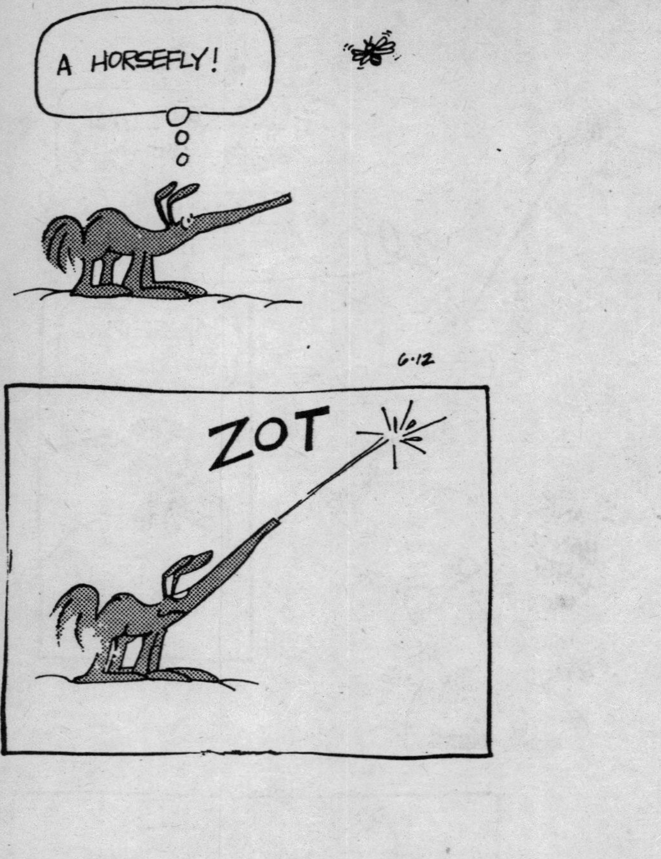
A HORSEFLY!
6·12
ZOT
PTUI

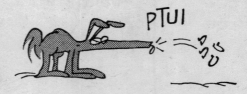

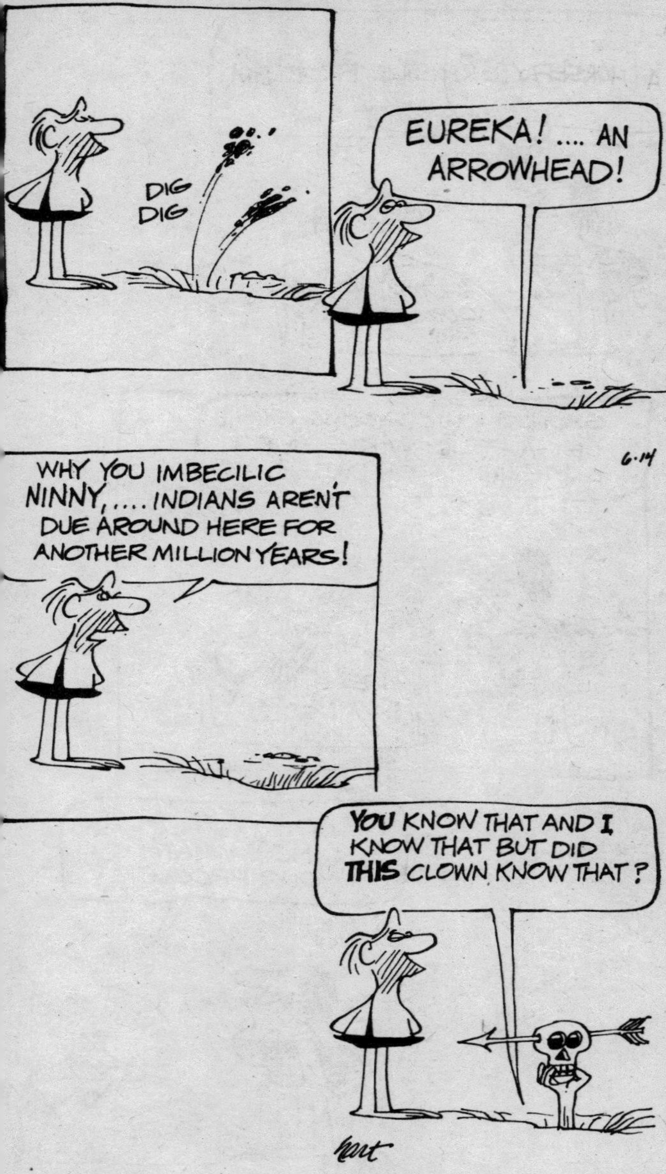
DIG
DIG
EUREKA! .... AN ARROWHEAD!
6·14
WHY YOU IMBECILIC NINNY, ... INDIANS AREN'T DUE AROUND HERE FOR ANOTHER MILLION YEARS!
YOU KNOW THAT AND I, KNOW THAT BUT DID THIS CLOWN KNOW THAT?
hart

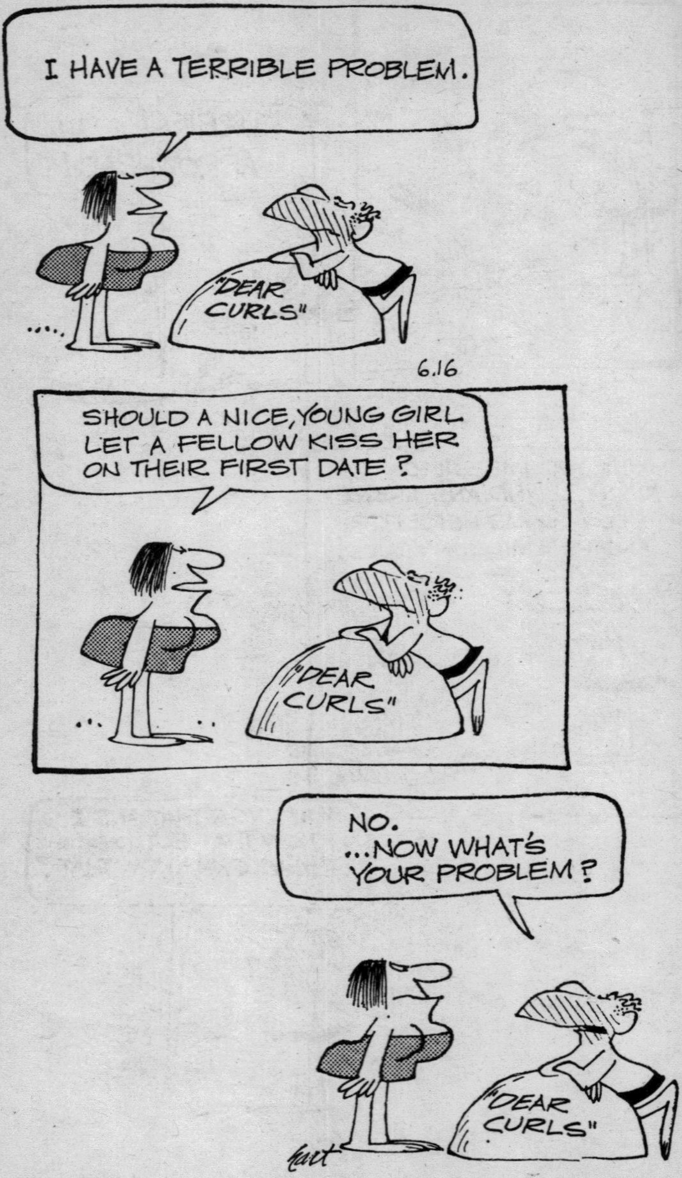
I HAVE A TERRIBLE PROBLEM.
"DEAR CURLS"
6.16
SHOULD A NICE, YOUNG GIRL LET A FELLOW KISS HER ON THEIR FIRST DATE?
"DEAR CURLS"
NO. ...NOW WHAT'S YOUR PROBLEM?
"DEAR CURLS"

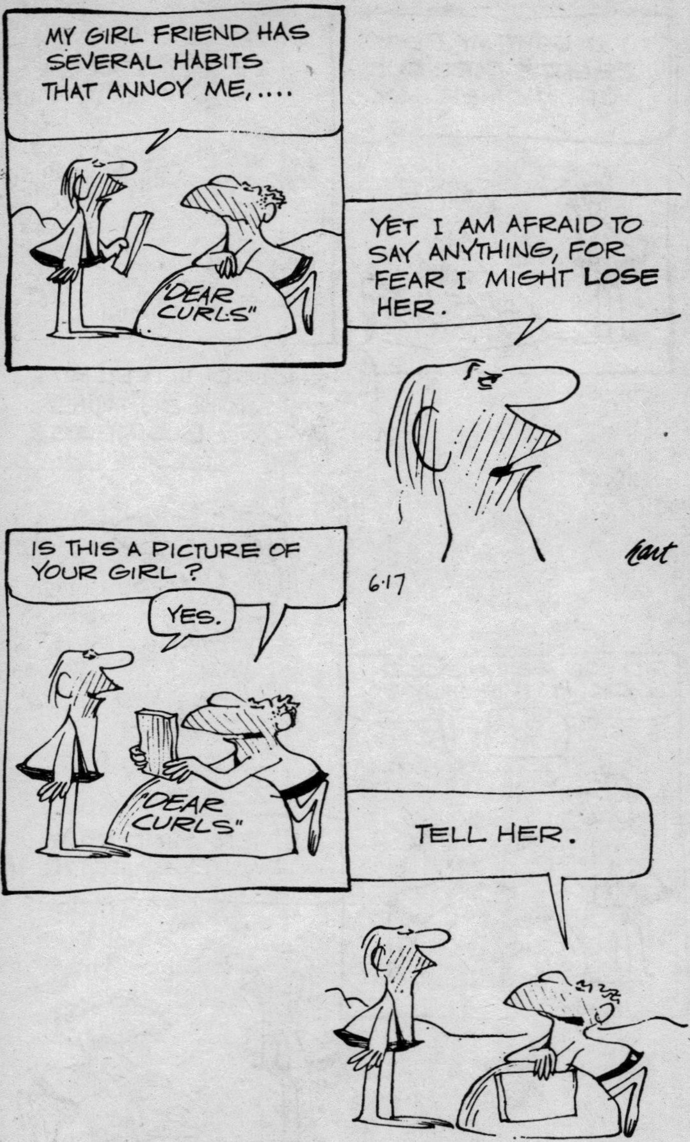
MY GIRL FRIEND HAS SEVERAL HABITS THAT ANNOY ME,....
"DEAR CURLS"
YET I AM AFRAID TO SAY ANYTHING, FOR FEAR I MIGHT LOSE HER.
hart
6·17
IS THIS A PICTURE OF YOUR GIRL?
YES.
"DEAR CURLS"
TELL HER.

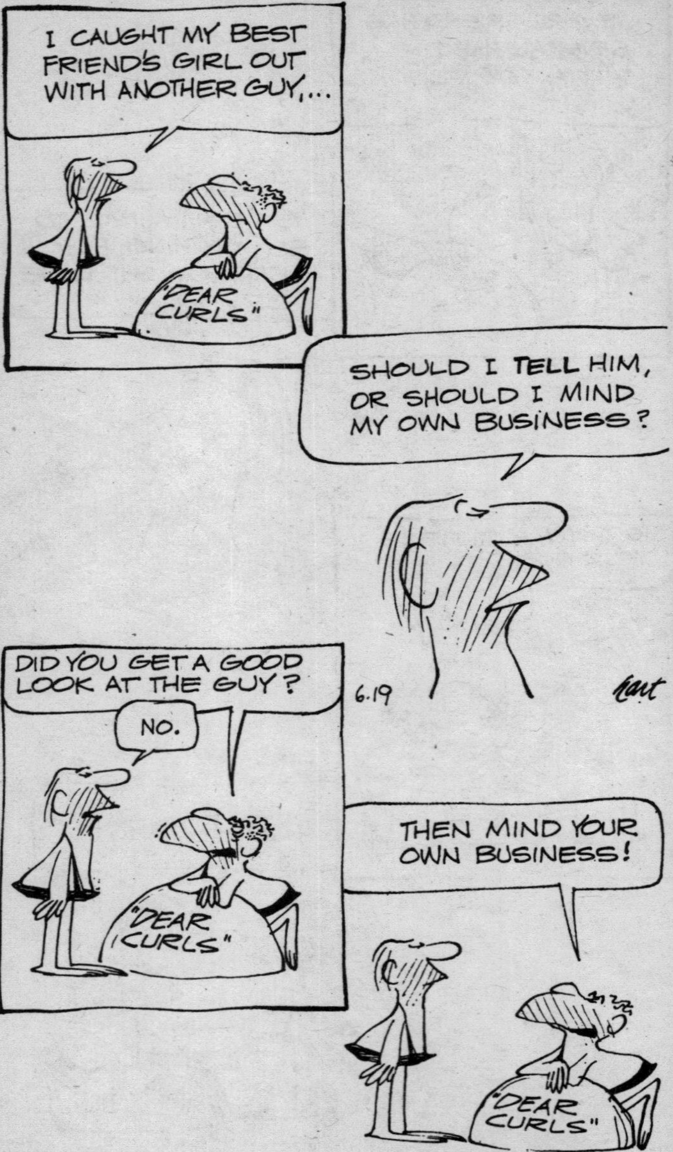
I CAUGHT MY BEST FRIEND'S GIRL OUT WITH ANOTHER GUY,...
"DEAR CURLS"
SHOULD I TELL HIM, OR SHOULD I MIND MY OWN BUSINESS?
6.19
hart
DID YOU GET A GOOD LOOK AT THE GUY?
NO.
"DEAR CURLS"
THEN MIND YOUR OWN BUSINESS!
"DEAR CURLS"

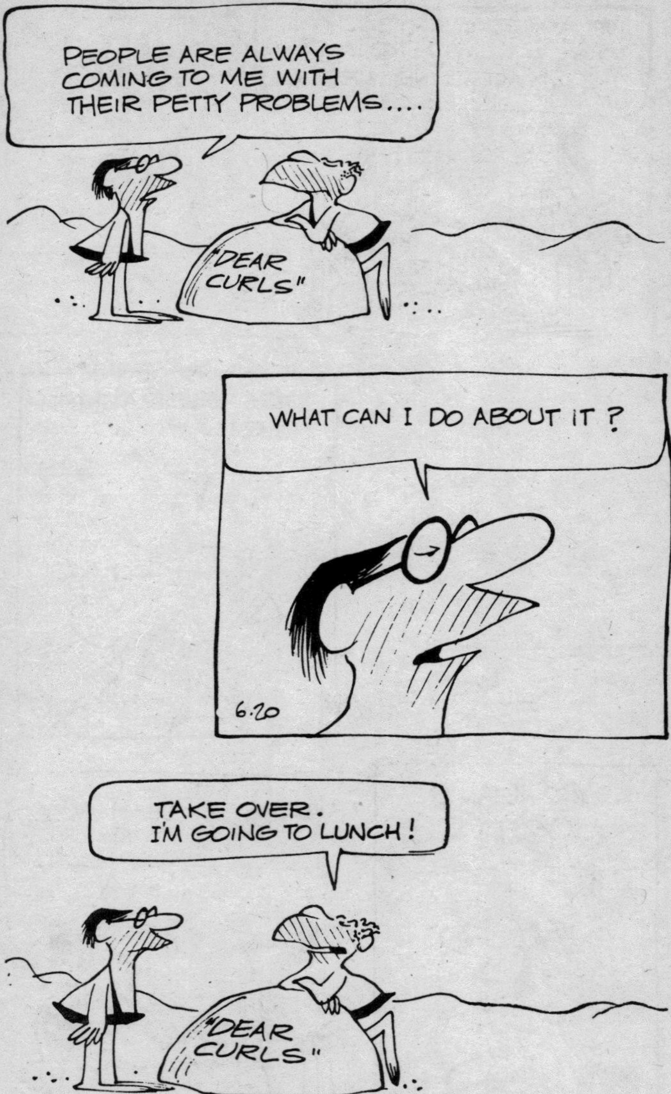
PEOPLE ARE ALWAYS COMING TO ME WITH THEIR PETTY PROBLEMS....
"DEAR CURLS"
WHAT CAN I DO ABOUT IT ?
6.20
TAKE OVER. I'M GOING TO LUNCH!
"DEAR CURLS"
hart

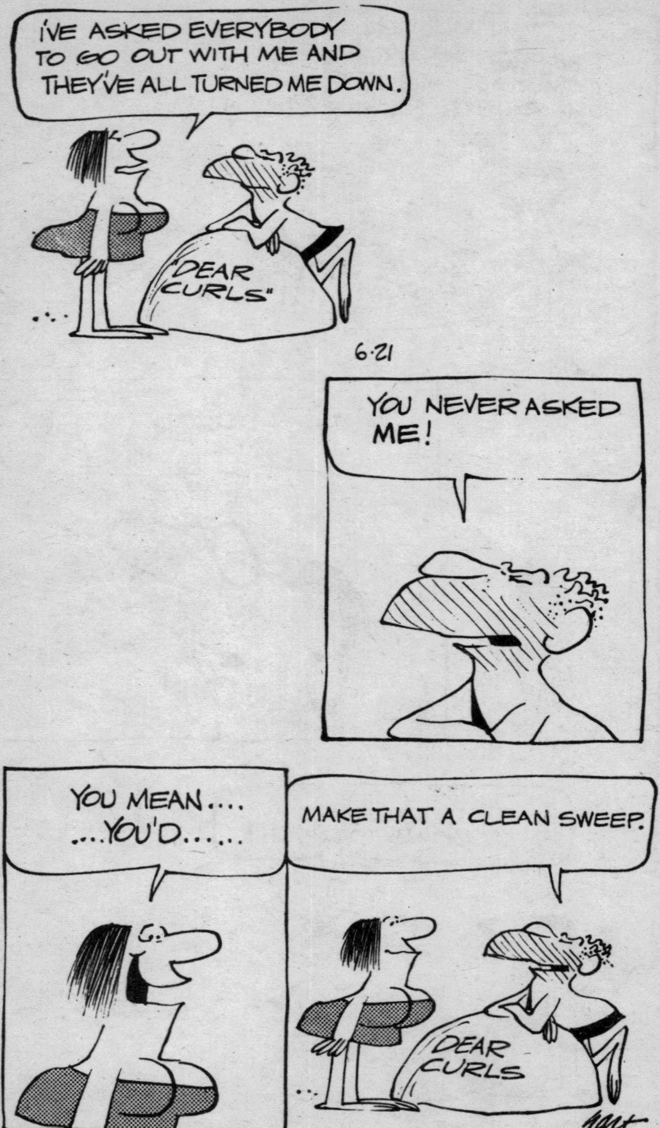
I'VE ASKED EVERYBODY TO GO OUT WITH ME AND THEY'VE ALL TURNED ME DOWN.
"DEAR CURLS"
6·21
YOU NEVER ASKED ME!
YOU MEAN.... ....YOU'D......
MAKE THAT A CLEAN SWEEP.
DEAR CURLS
hart

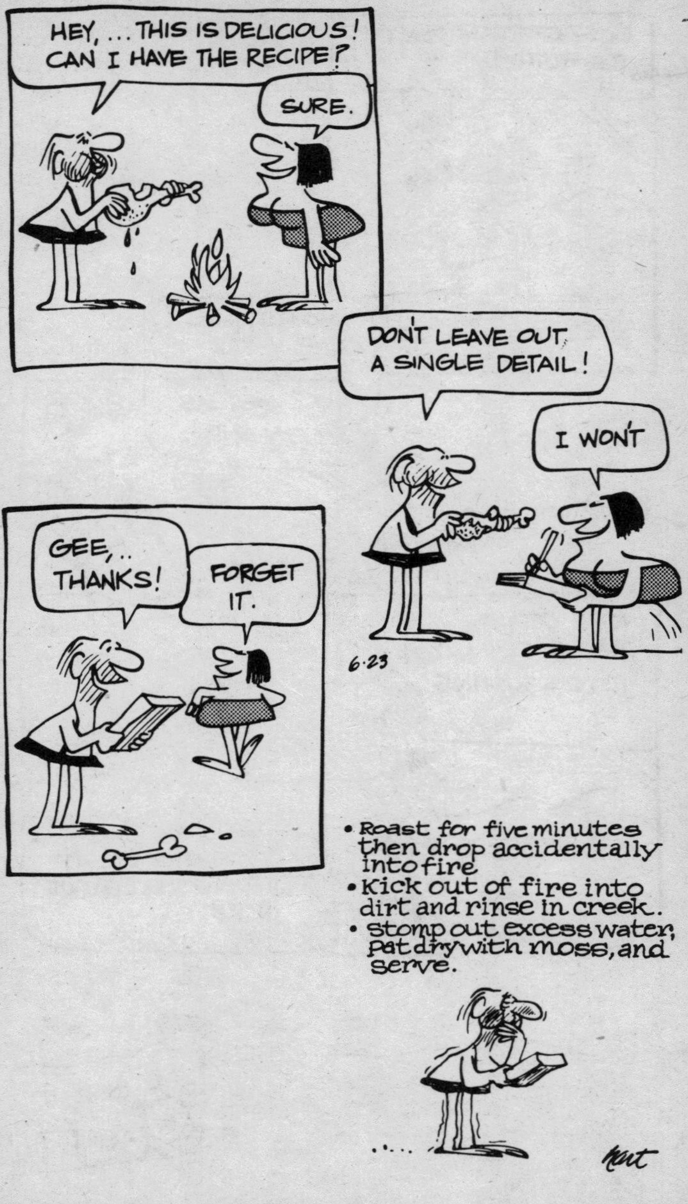
HEY, ... THIS IS DELICIOUS! CAN I HAVE THE RECIPE?
SURE.
DON'T LEAVE OUT A SINGLE DETAIL!
I WON'T
6·23
GEE, .. THANKS!
FORGET IT.
• Roast for five minutes then drop accidentally into fire
• Kick out of fire into dirt and rinse in creek.
• Stomp out excess water, pat dry with moss, and serve.
hart

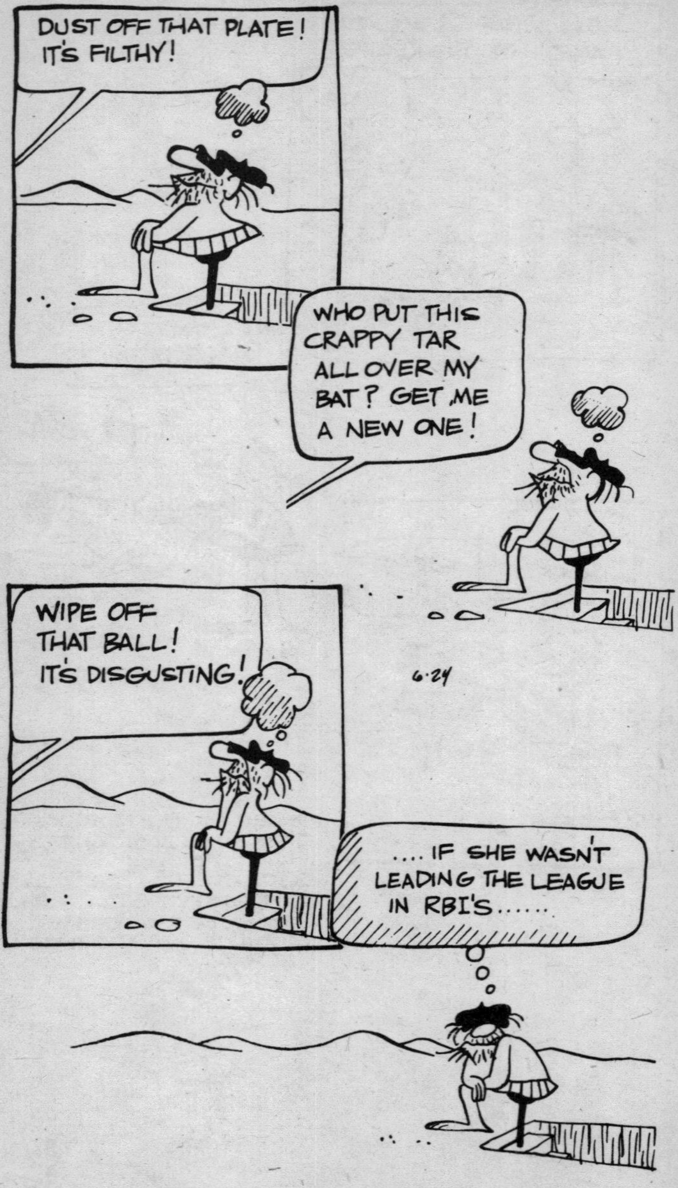
DUST OFF THAT PLATE! IT'S FILTHY!
WHO PUT THIS CRAPPY TAR ALL OVER MY BAT? GET ME A NEW ONE!
WIPE OFF THAT BALL! IT'S DISGUSTING!
6·24
....IF SHE WASN'T LEADING THE LEAGUE IN RBI'S......

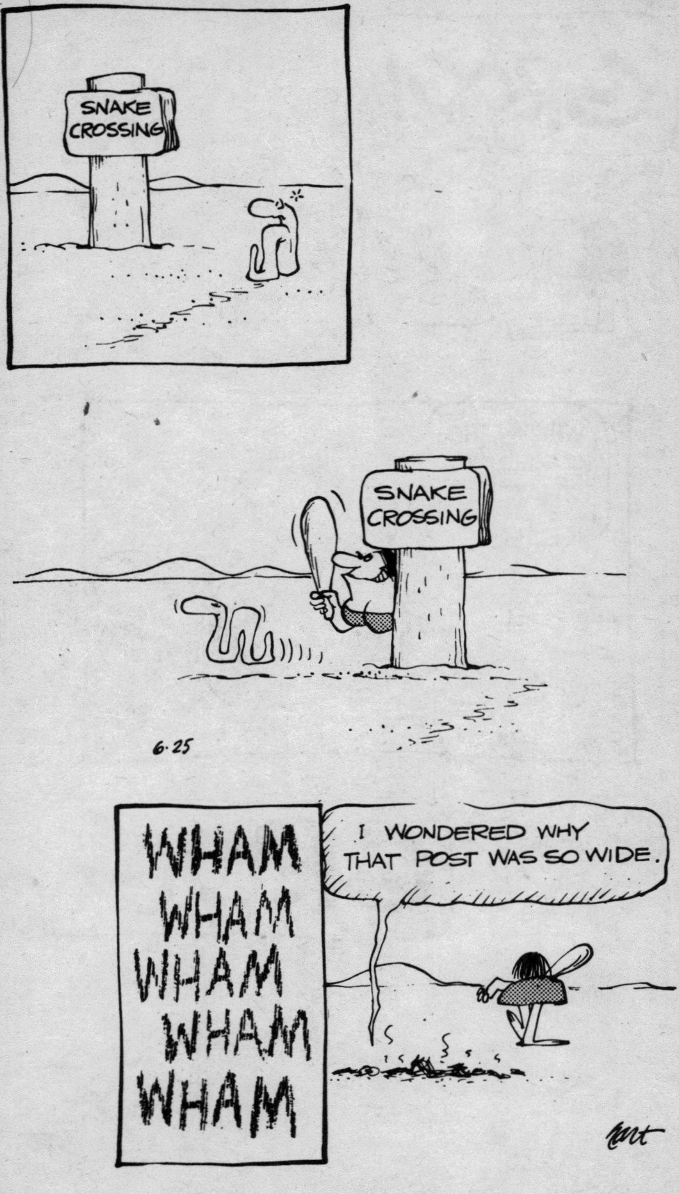
SNAKE CROSSING
SNAKE CROSSING
6·25
WHAM
WHAM
WHAM
WHAM
WHAM
I WONDERED WHY THAT POST WAS SO WIDE.

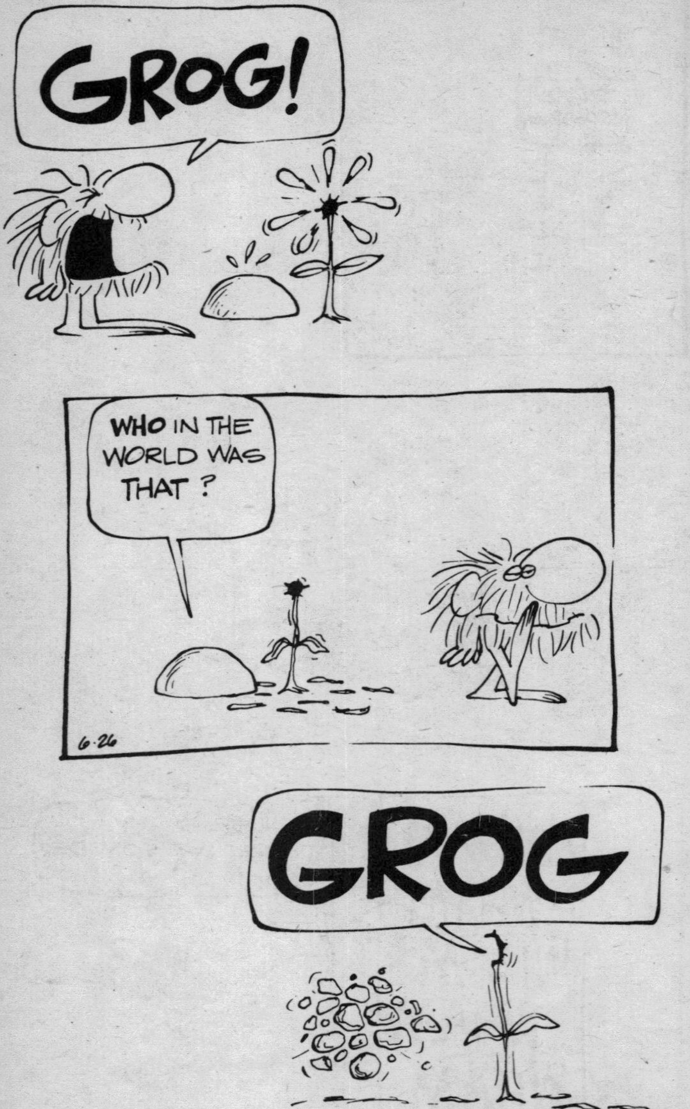
GROG!
WHO IN THE WORLD WAS THAT ?
6·26
GROG
hart

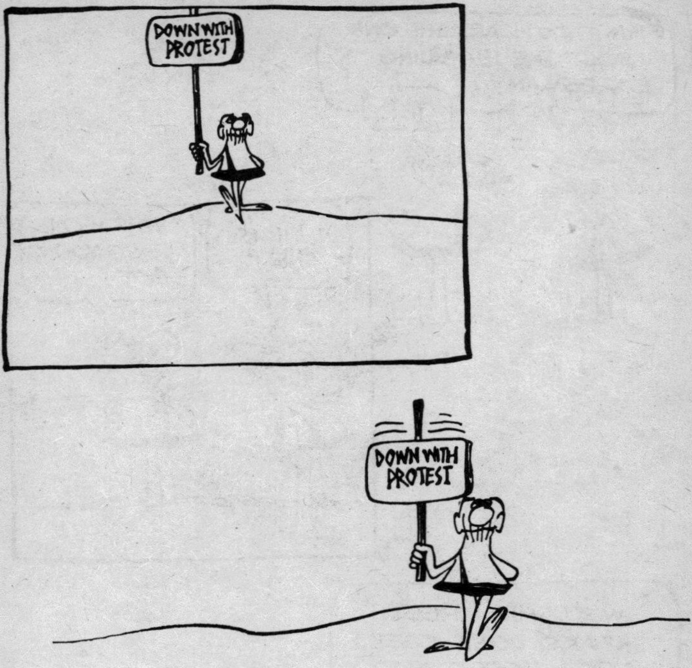
DOWN WITH PROTEST
DOWN WITH PROTEST

6·27

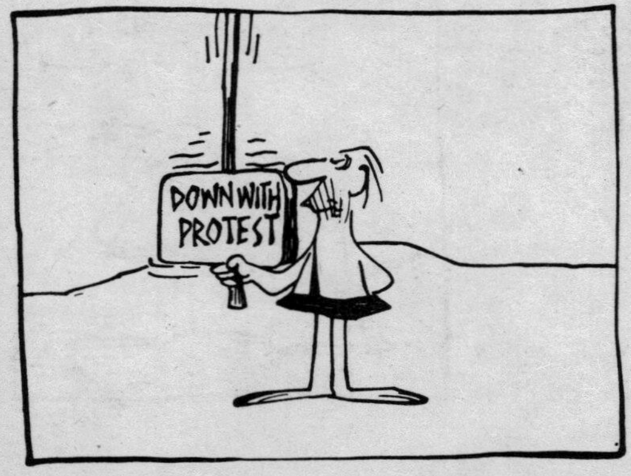
DOWN WITH PROTEST

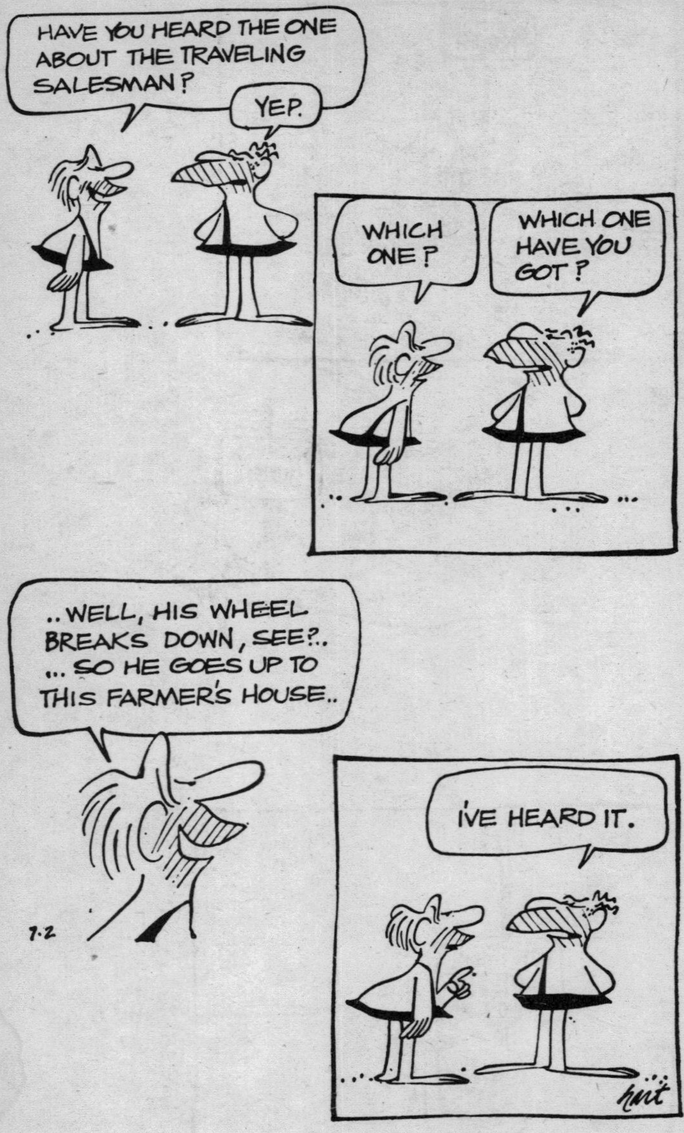
HAVE YOU HEARD THE ONE ABOUT THE TRAVELING SALESMAN?
YEP.
WHICH ONE?
WHICH ONE HAVE YOU GOT?
..WELL, HIS WHEEL BREAKS DOWN, SEE?.. ...SO HE GOES UP TO THIS FARMER'S HOUSE..
I'VE HEARD IT.
7-2
hart

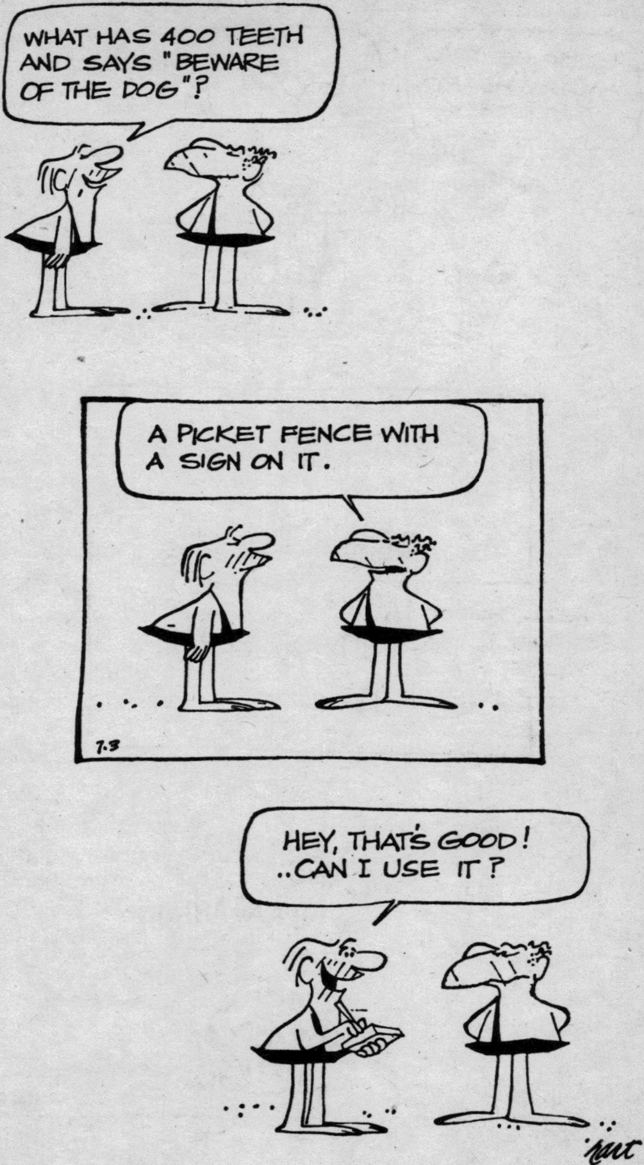
WHAT HAS 400 TEETH AND SAYS "BEWARE OF THE DOG"?
A PICKET FENCE WITH A SIGN ON IT.
7-3
HEY, THAT'S GOOD! ..CAN I USE IT?

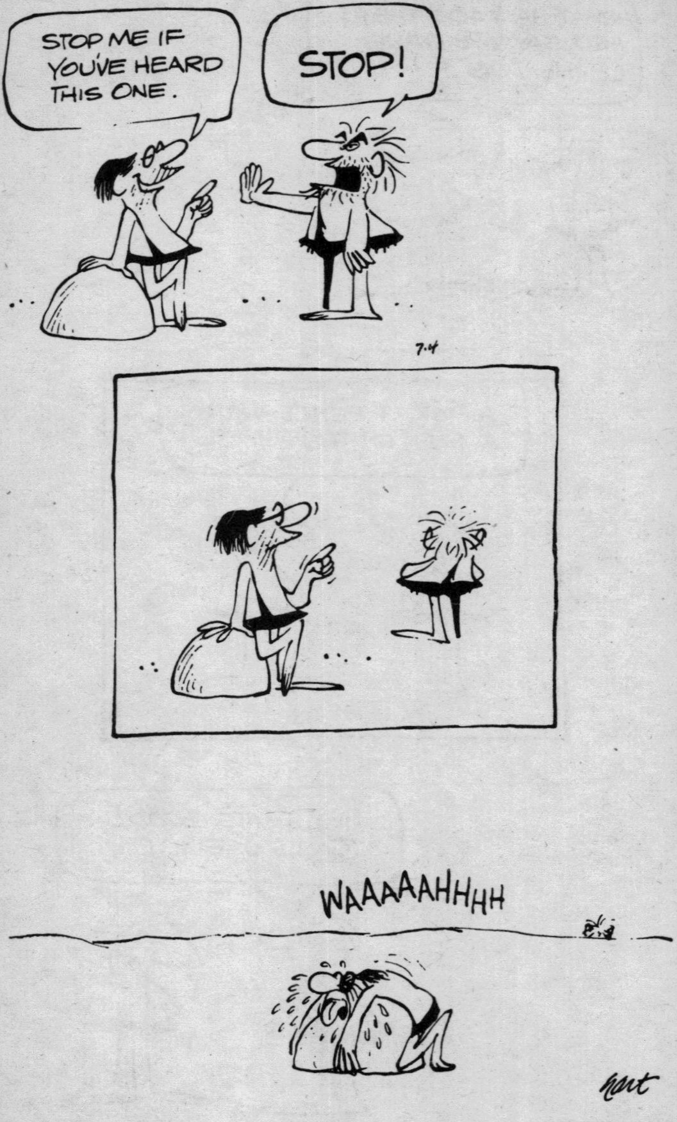
STOP ME IF YOU'VE HEARD THIS ONE.
STOP!
WAAAAAHHHH
hart

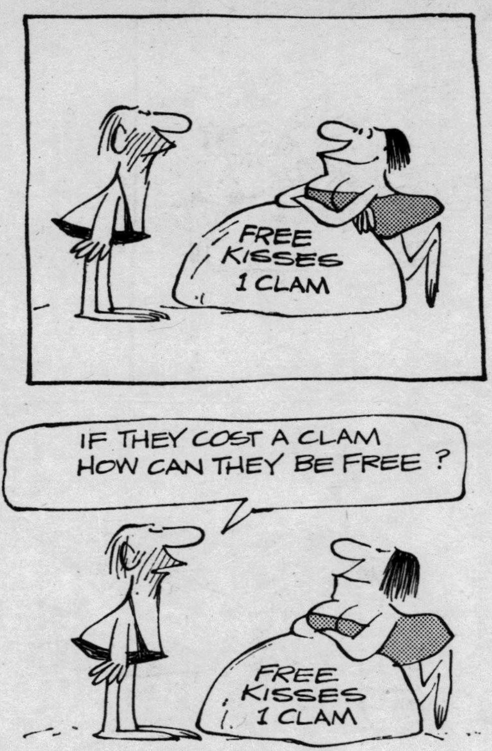
FREE
KISSES
1 CLAM
IF THEY COST A CLAM
HOW CAN THEY BE FREE ?
FREE
KISSES
1 CLAM

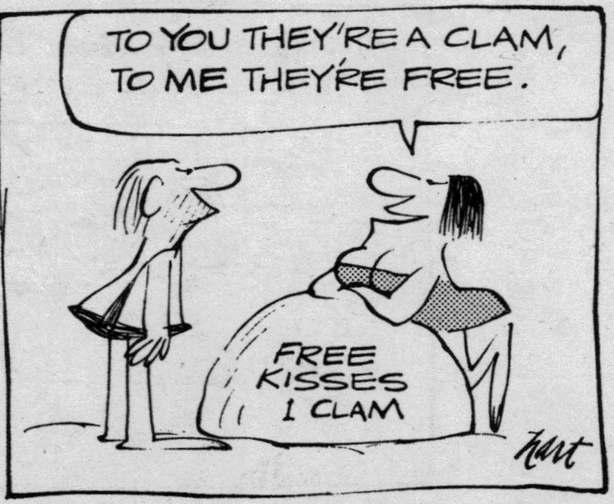
TO YOU THEY'RE A CLAM,
TO ME THEY'RE FREE.
FREE
KISSES
1 CLAM
hart

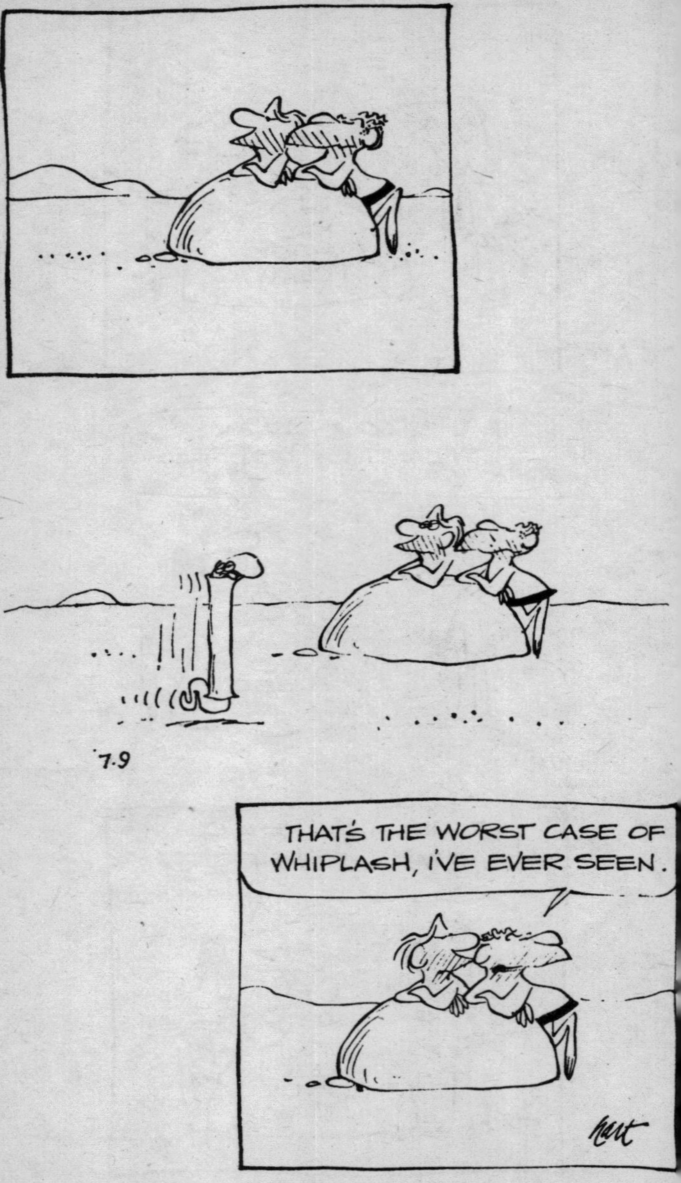
7-9
THAT'S THE WORST CASE OF WHIPLASH, I'VE EVER SEEN.
hart

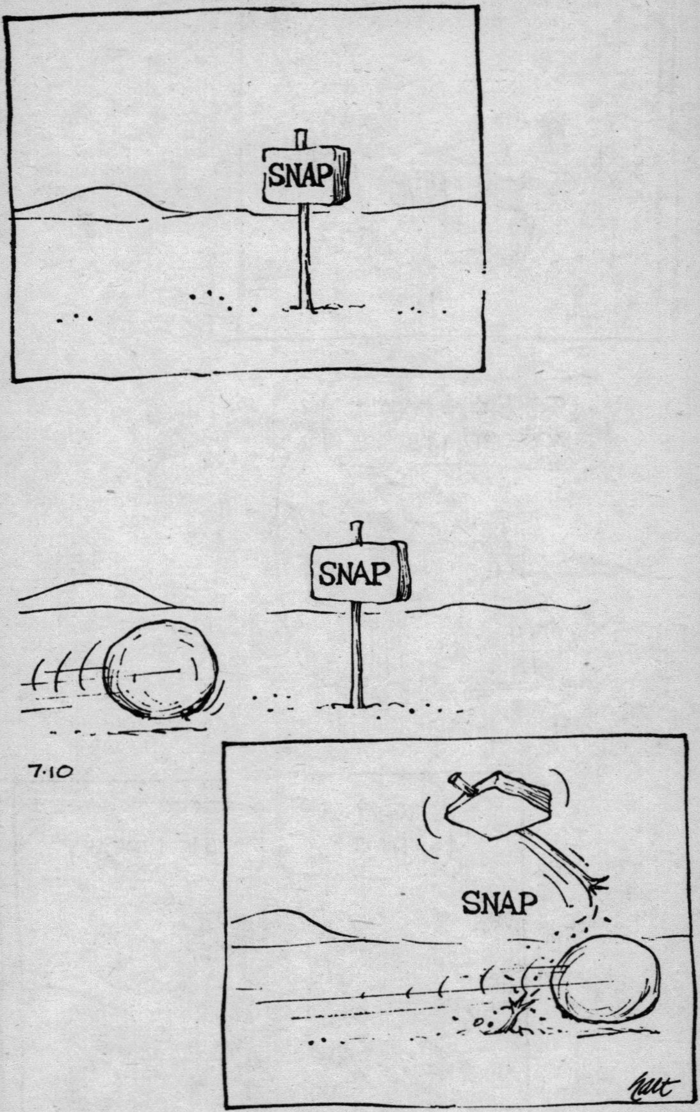
SNAP
SNAP
7·10
SNAP

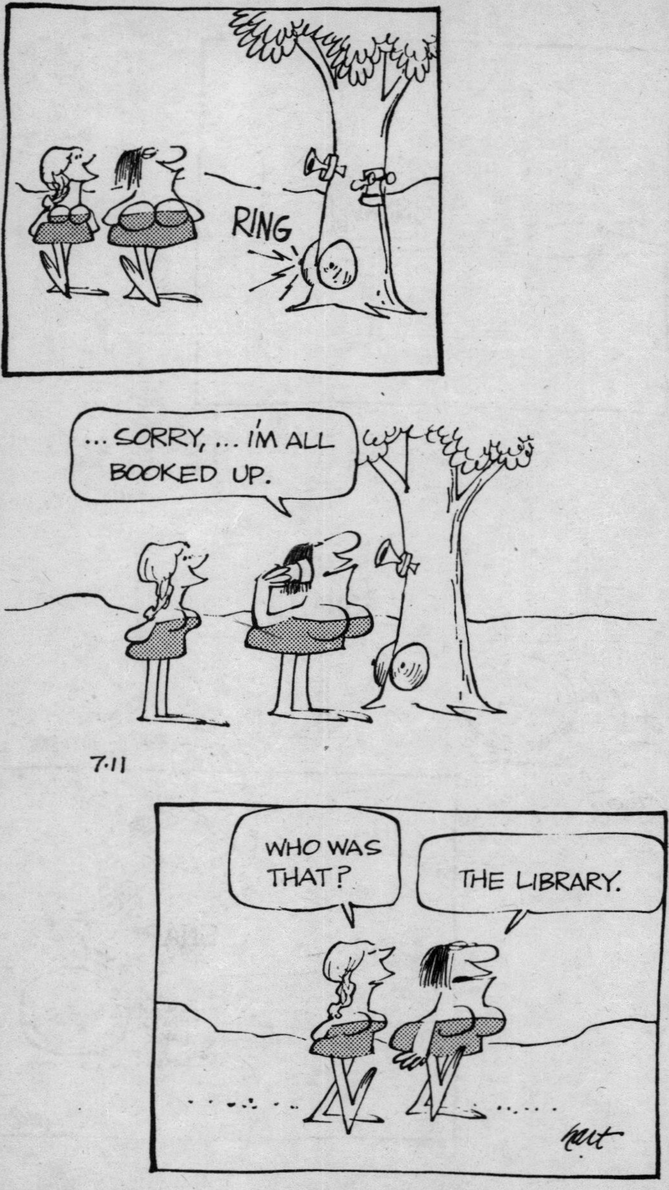
RING
... SORRY, ... I'M ALL BOOKED UP.
7·11
WHO WAS THAT?
THE LIBRARY.

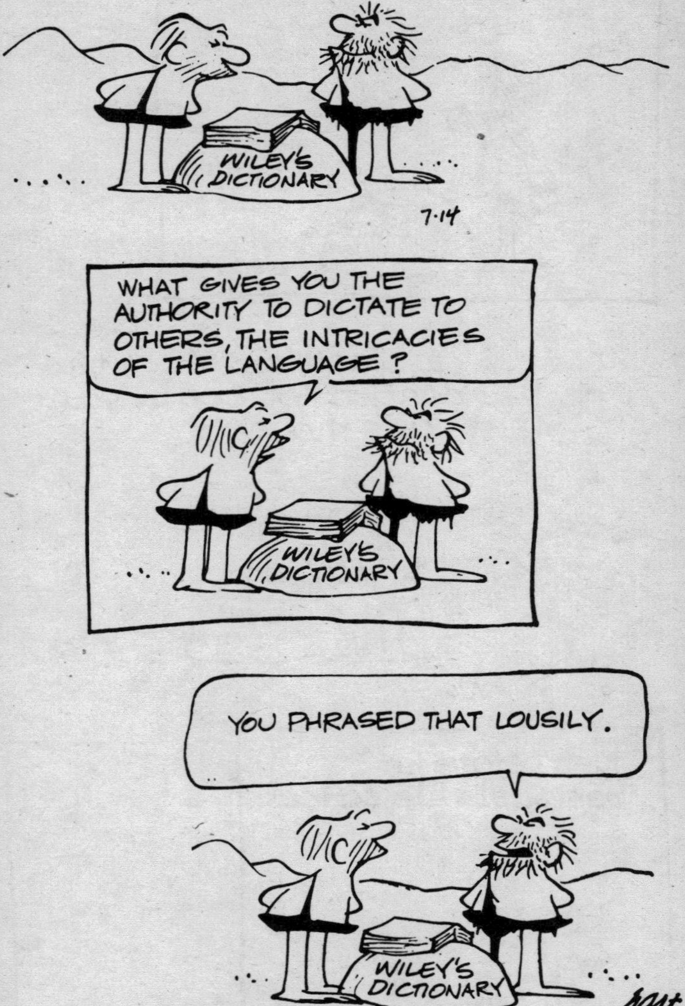
WILEY'S DICTIONARY
7·14
WHAT GIVES YOU THE AUTHORITY TO DICTATE TO OTHERS, THE INTRICACIES OF THE LANGUAGE?
WILEY'S DICTIONARY
YOU PHRASED THAT LOUSILY.
WILEY'S DICTIONARY
hart

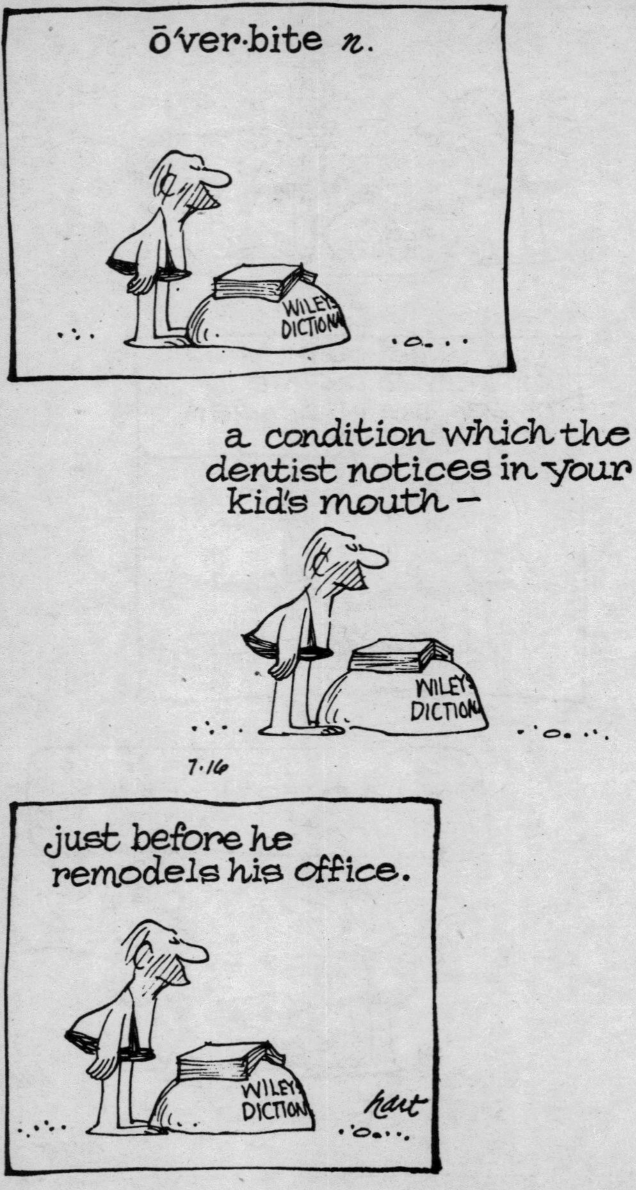
ō'ver·bite *n.*
a condition which the dentist notices in your kid's mouth –
7·16
just before he remodels his office.
hart

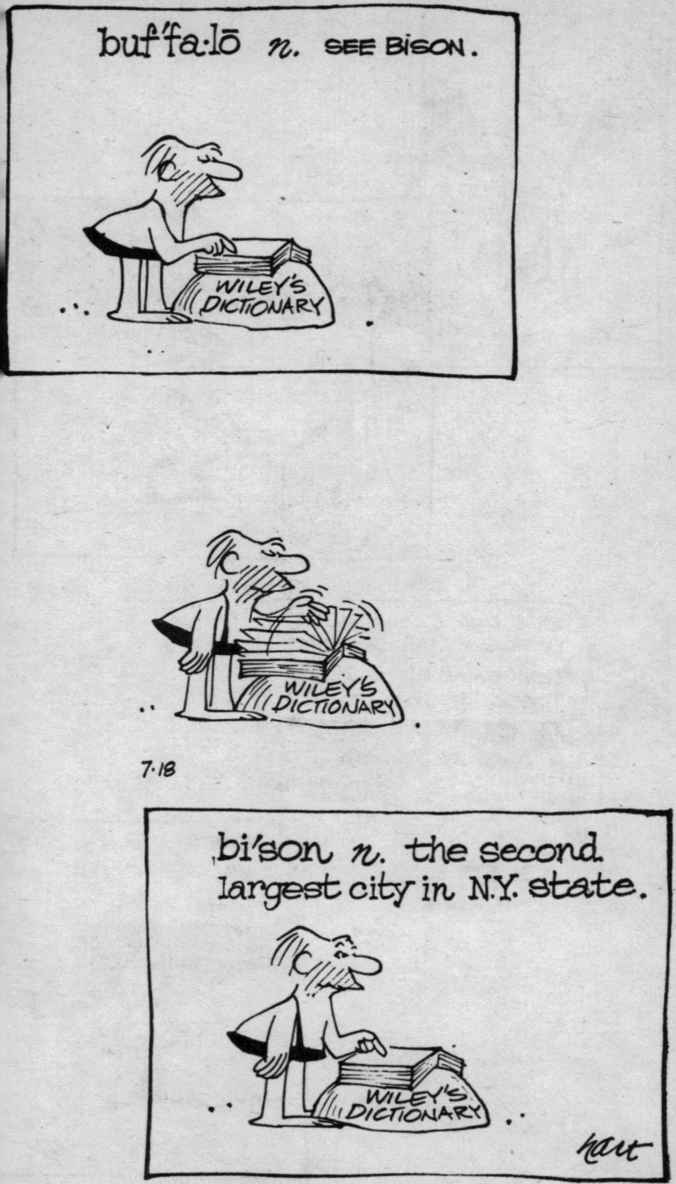
buf'fa·lō n. SEE BISON.
WILEY'S DICTIONARY
WILEY'S DICTIONARY
7·18
bi'son n. the second largest city in N.Y. state.
WILEY'S DICTIONARY
hart

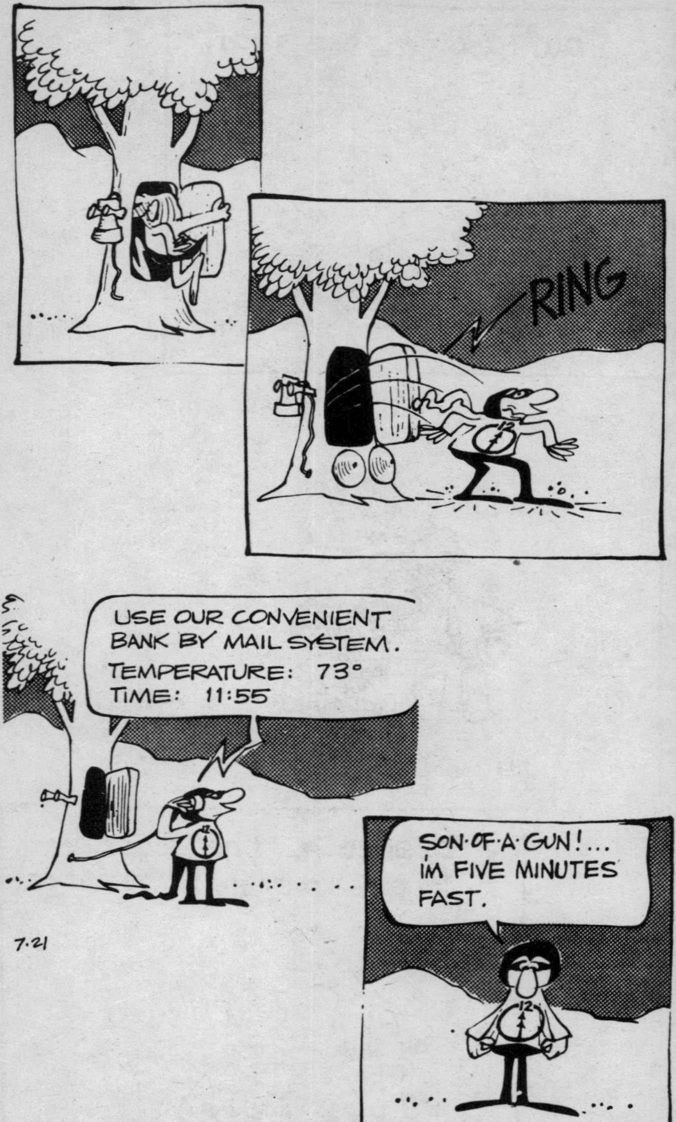
RING
USE OUR CONVENIENT BANK BY MAIL SYSTEM. TEMPERATURE: 73° TIME: 11:55
7·21
SON·OF·A·GUN!... IM FIVE MINUTES FAST.
hart

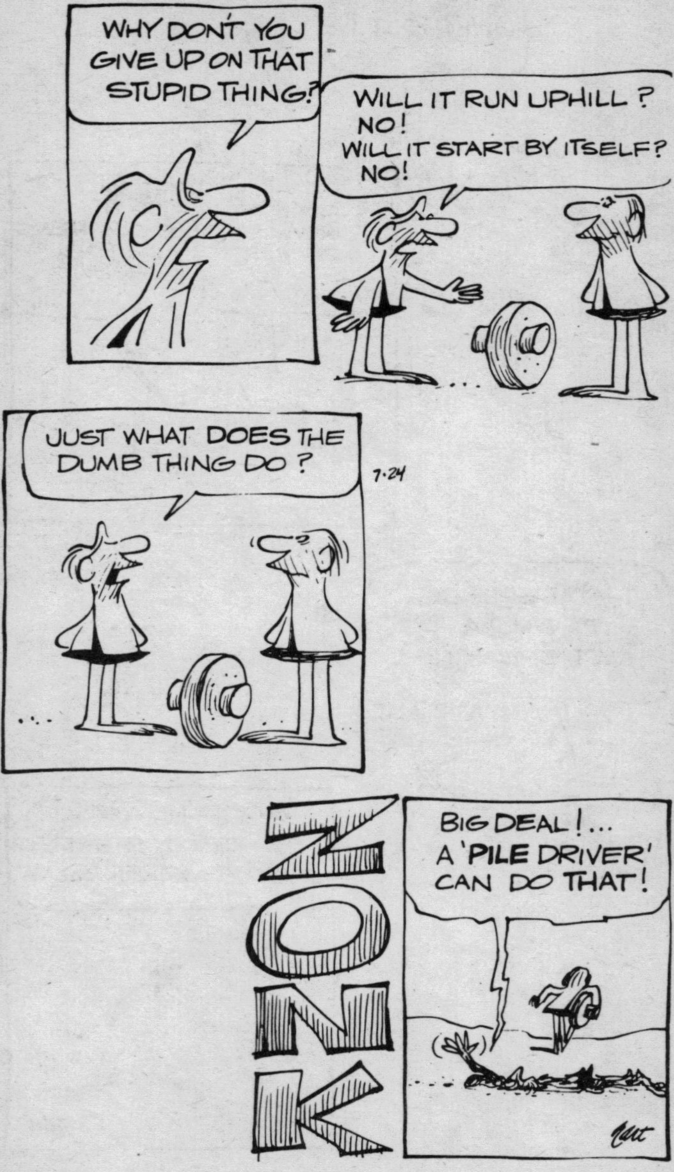
WHY DON'T YOU GIVE UP ON THAT STUPID THING?
WILL IT RUN UPHILL? NO! WILL IT START BY ITSELF? NO!
JUST WHAT DOES THE DUMB THING DO?
7·24
ZONK
BIG DEAL!... A 'PILE DRIVER' CAN DO THAT!

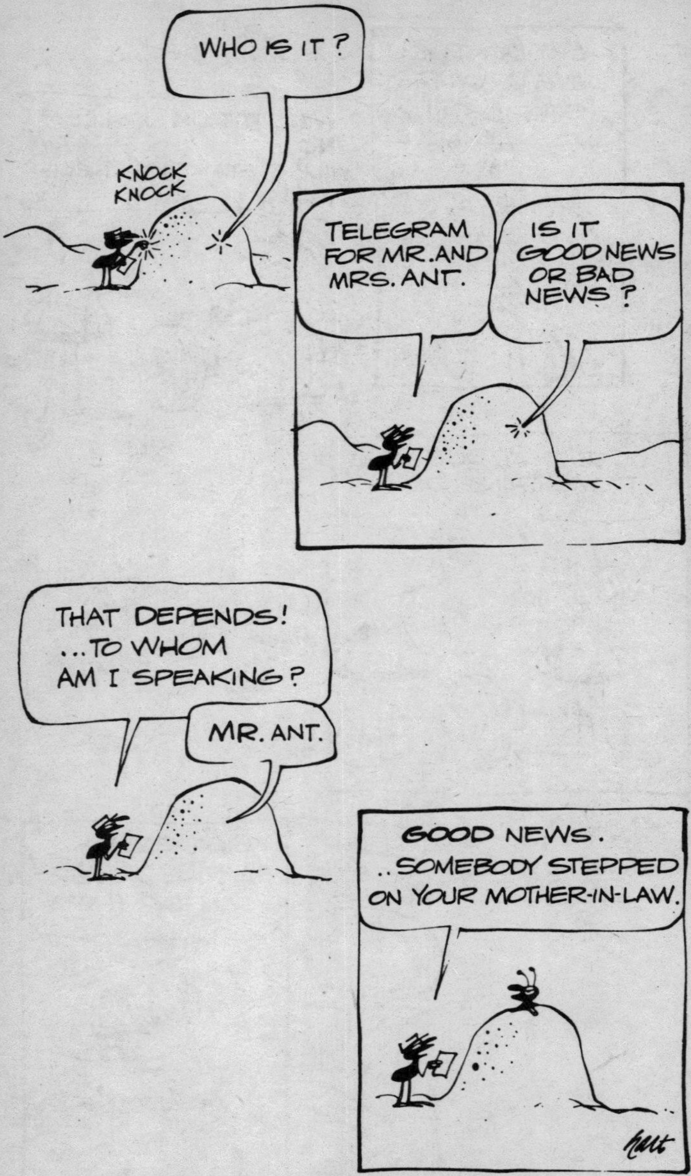

WHO IS IT?
KNOCK KNOCK
TELEGRAM FOR MR. AND MRS. ANT.
IS IT GOOD NEWS OR BAD NEWS?
THAT DEPENDS! ...TO WHOM AM I SPEAKING?
MR. ANT.
GOOD NEWS. ..SOMEBODY STEPPED ON YOUR MOTHER-IN-LAW.
hart

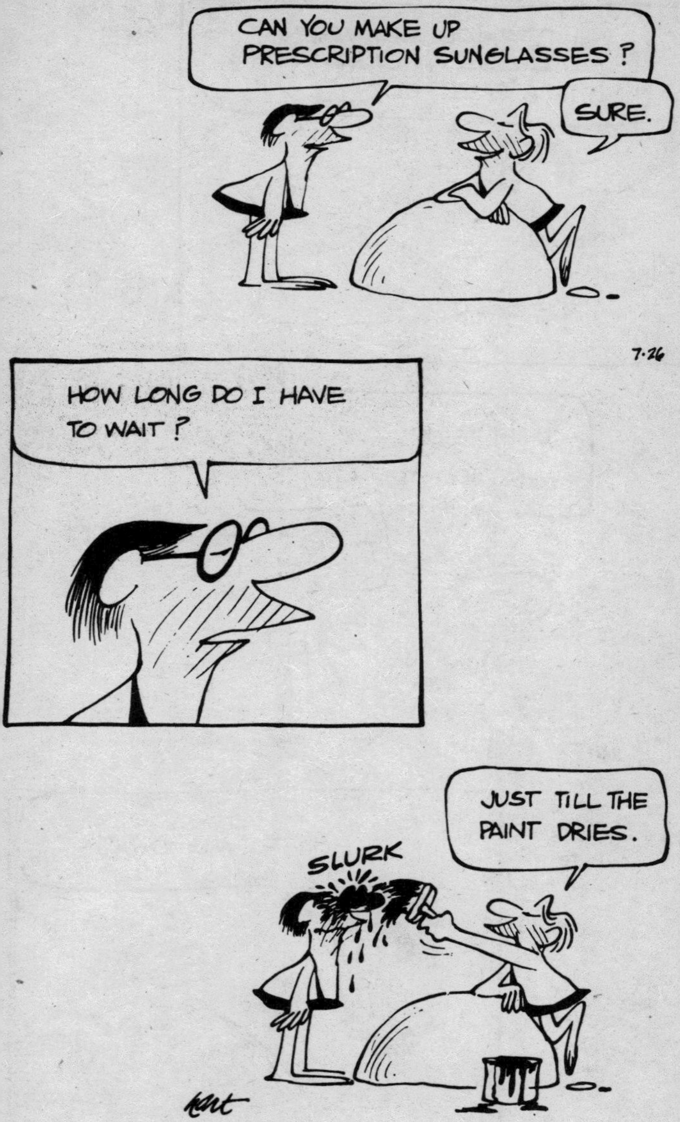
CAN YOU MAKE UP PRESCRIPTION SUNGLASSES?
SURE.
7·26
HOW LONG DO I HAVE TO WAIT?
SLURK
JUST TILL THE PAINT DRIES.

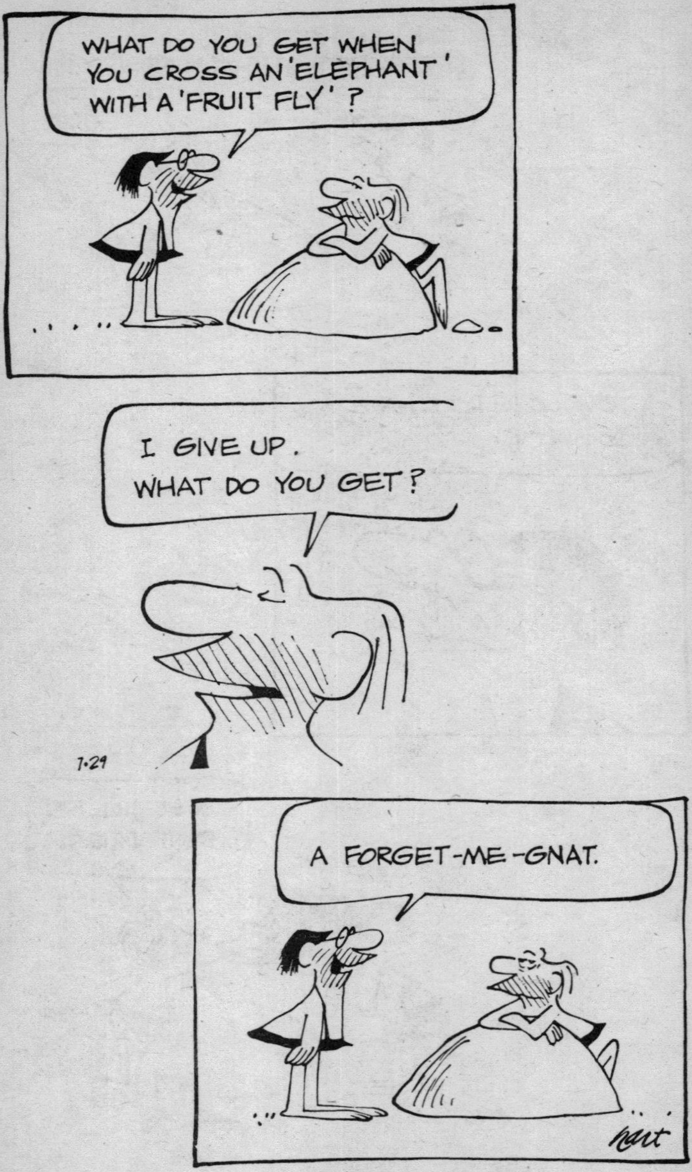
WHAT DO YOU GET WHEN YOU CROSS AN 'ELEPHANT' WITH A 'FRUIT FLY' ?
I GIVE UP. WHAT DO YOU GET?
7·29
A FORGET-ME-GNAT.
hart

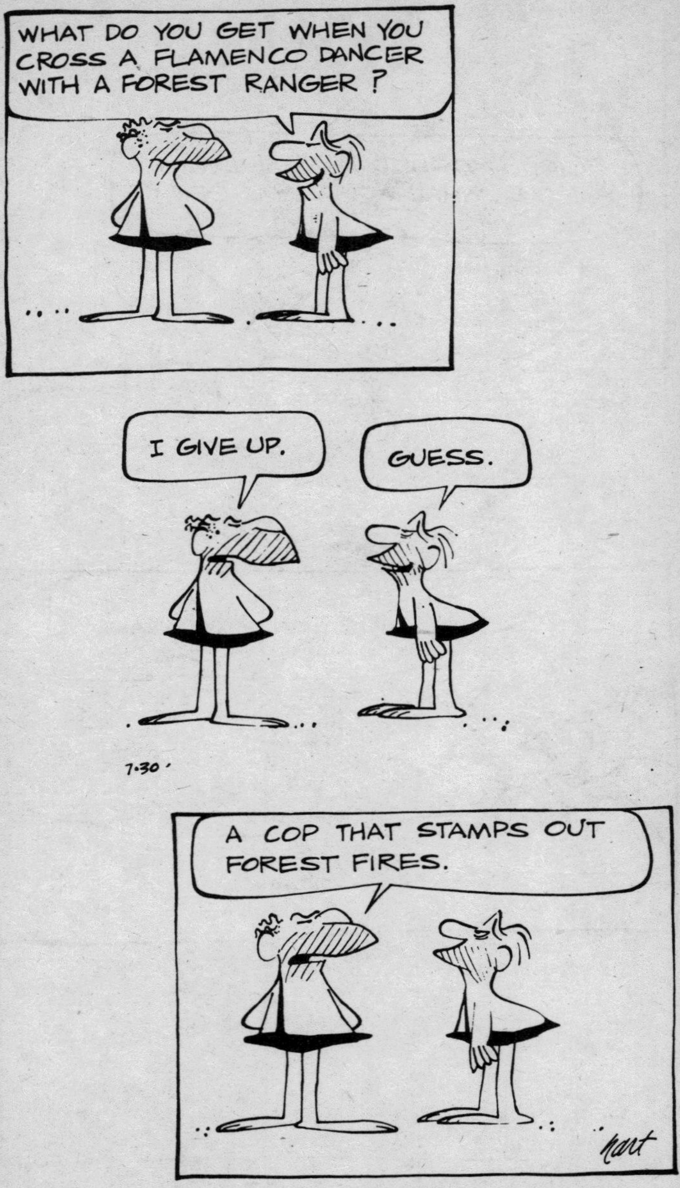
WHAT DO YOU GET WHEN YOU CROSS A FLAMENCO DANCER WITH A FOREST RANGER?
I GIVE UP.
GUESS.
7·30
A COP THAT STAMPS OUT FOREST FIRES.
hart

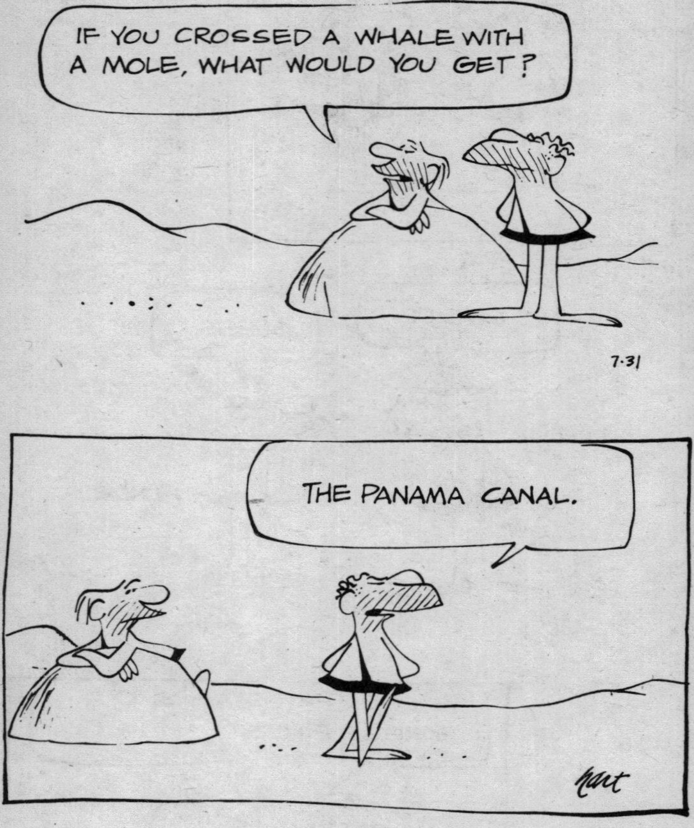
IF YOU CROSSED A WHALE WITH A MOLE, WHAT WOULD YOU GET?
7·31
THE PANAMA CANAL.
hart

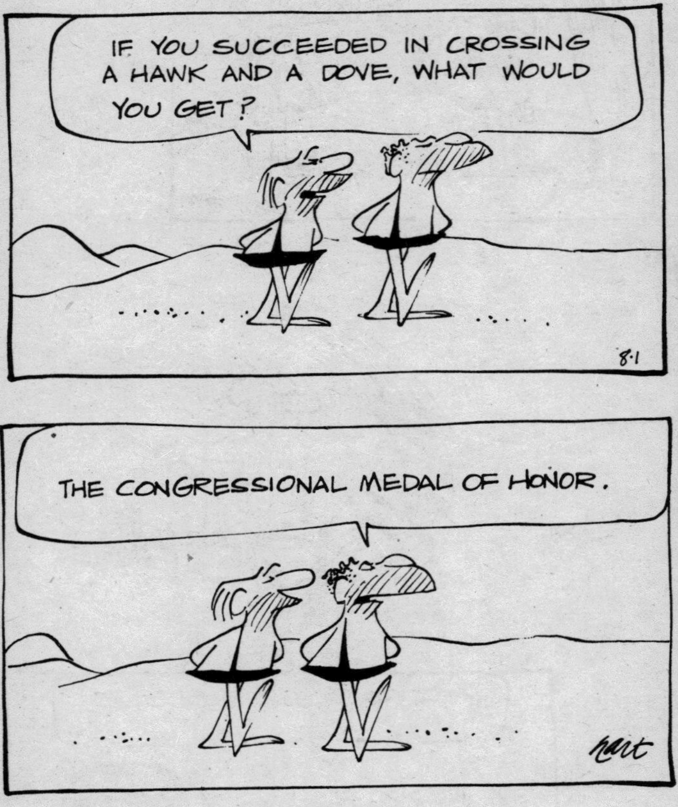
IF YOU SUCCEEDED IN CROSSING A HAWK AND A DOVE, WHAT WOULD YOU GET?
8·1
THE CONGRESSIONAL MEDAL OF HONOR.
hart

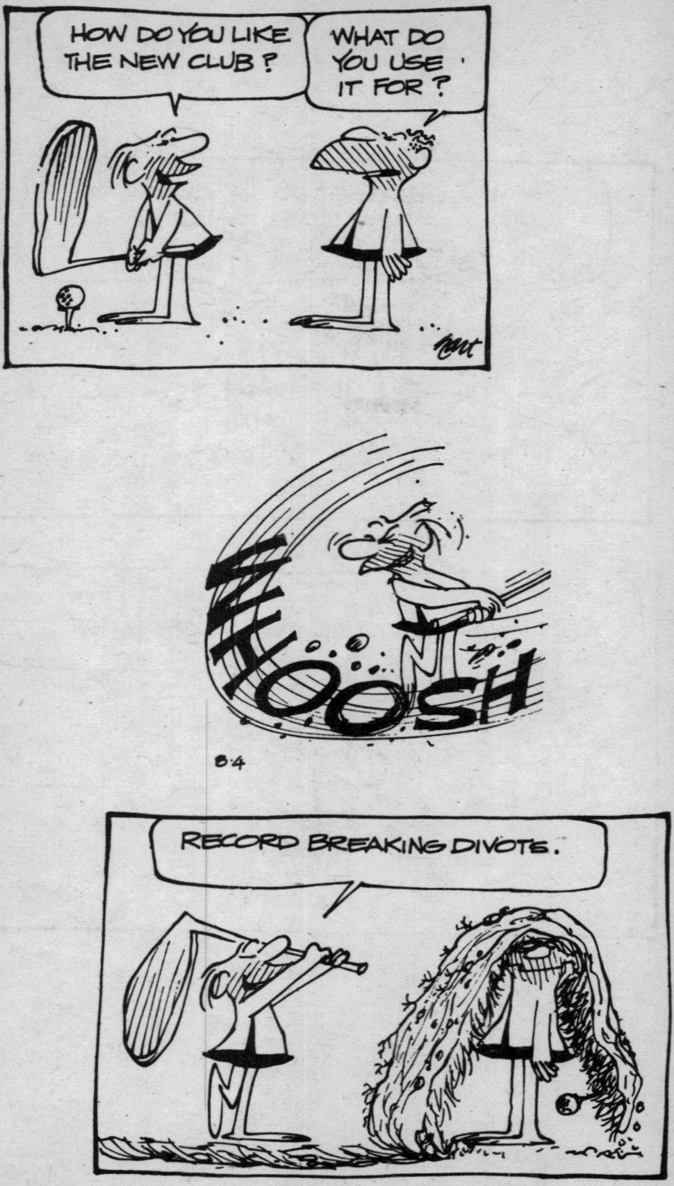
HOW DO YOU LIKE THE NEW CLUB?
WHAT DO YOU USE IT FOR?
WHOOSH
8·4
RECORD BREAKING DIVOTS.

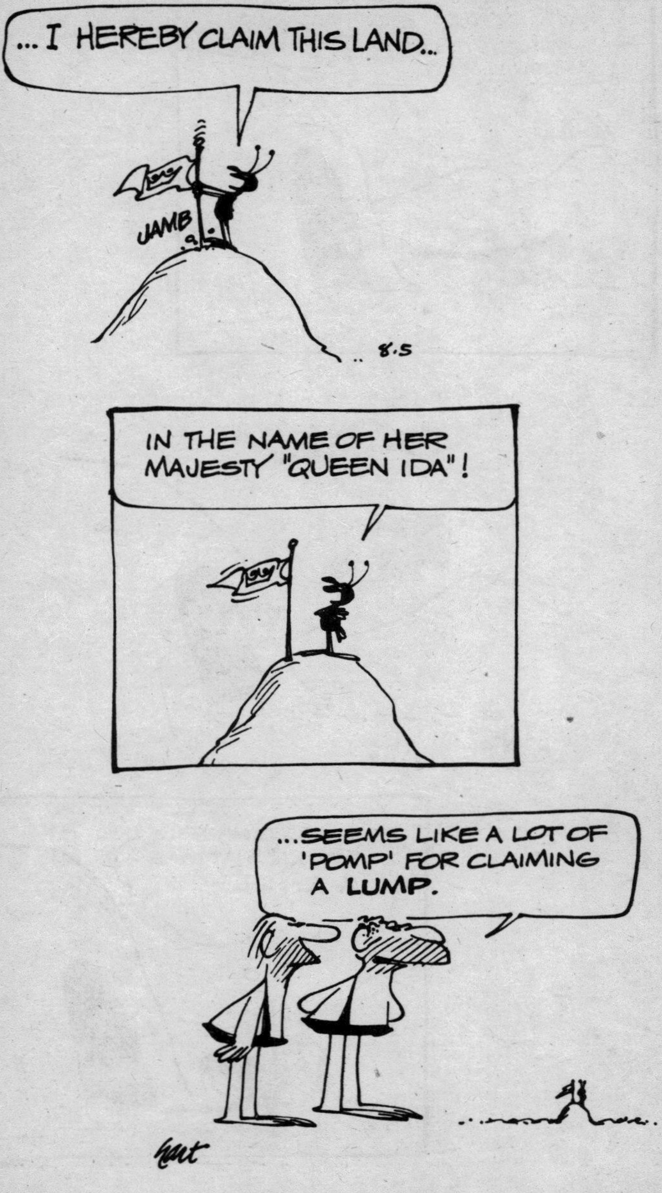
...I HEREBY CLAIM THIS LAND...
JAMB
IN THE NAME OF HER MAJESTY "QUEEN IDA"!
...SEEMS LIKE A LOT OF 'POMP' FOR CLAIMING A **LUMP**.

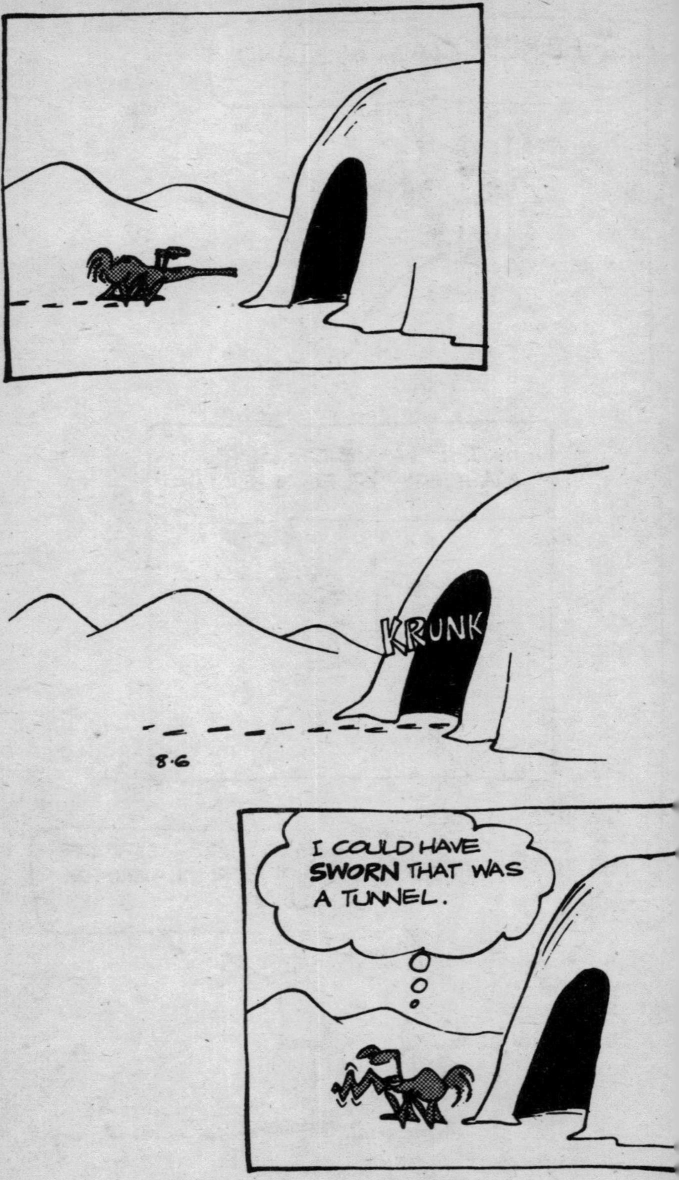
KRUNK
8·6
I COULD HAVE SWORN THAT WAS A TUNNEL.

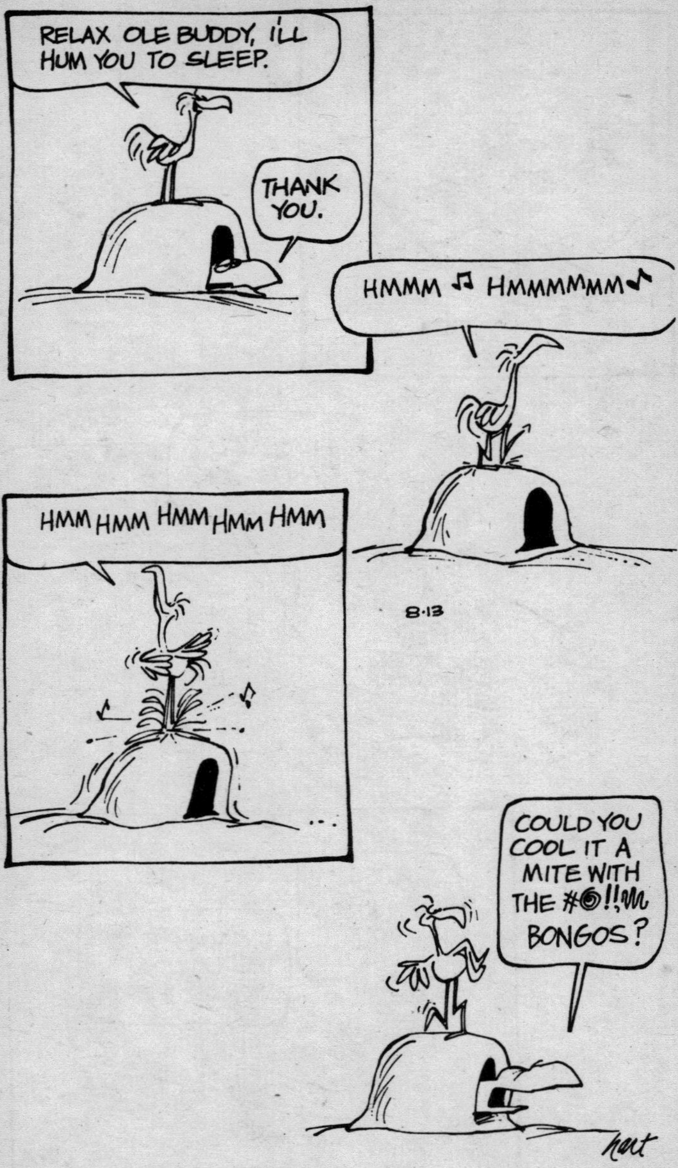
RELAX OLE BUDDY, I'LL HUM YOU TO SLEEP.
THANK YOU.
HMMM ♫ HMMMMMM ♪
HMM HMM HMM HMM HMM
COULD YOU COOL IT A MITE WITH THE #@!!,m BONGOS?
8·13
hart

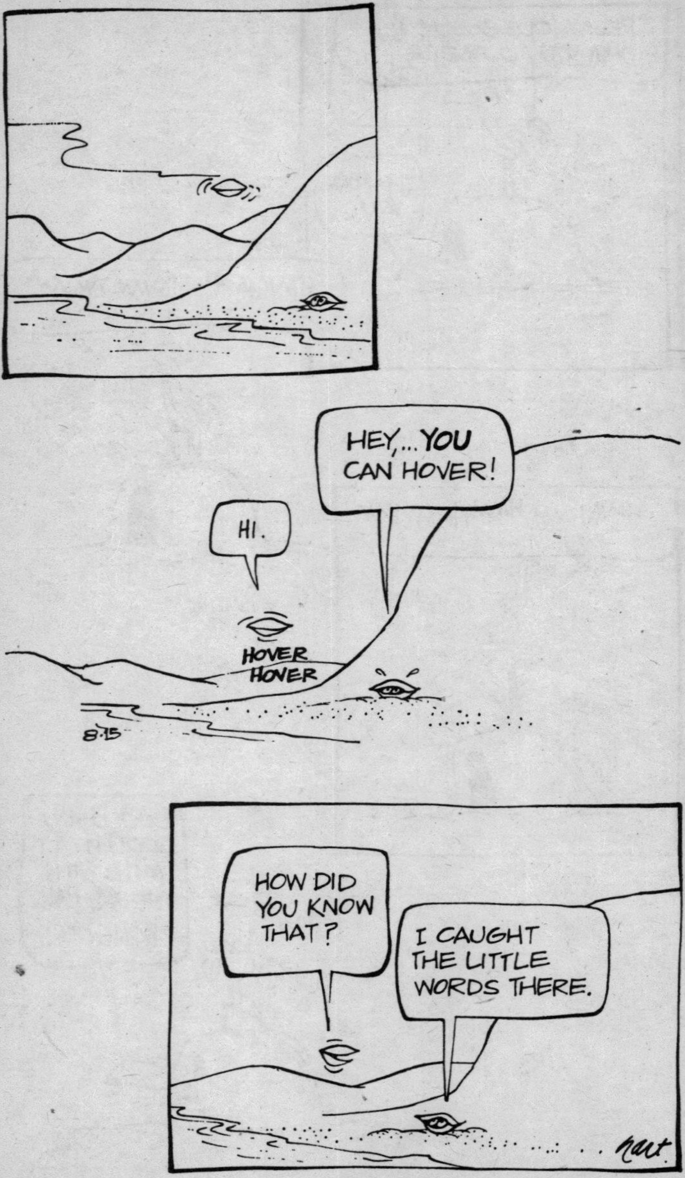
HI.
HEY,... YOU CAN HOVER!
HOVER
HOVER
8·15
HOW DID YOU KNOW THAT?
I CAUGHT THE LITTLE WORDS THERE.

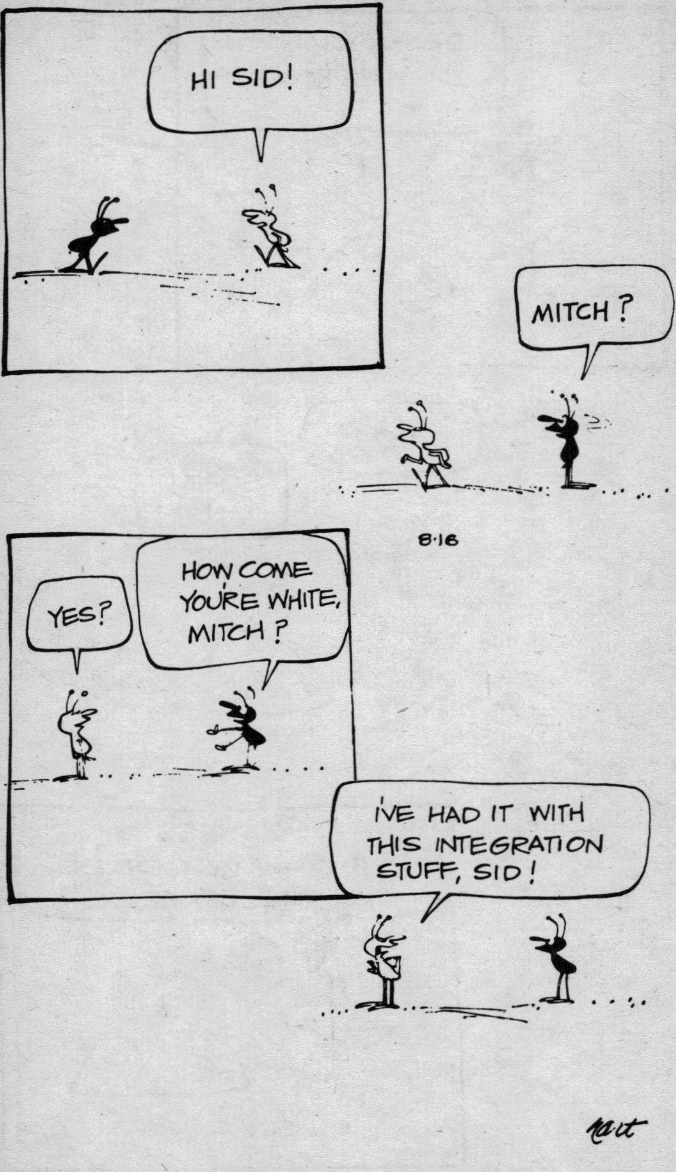
HI SID!
MITCH?
8·16
YES?
HOW COME YOU'RE WHITE, MITCH?
I'VE HAD IT WITH THIS INTEGRATION STUFF, SID!

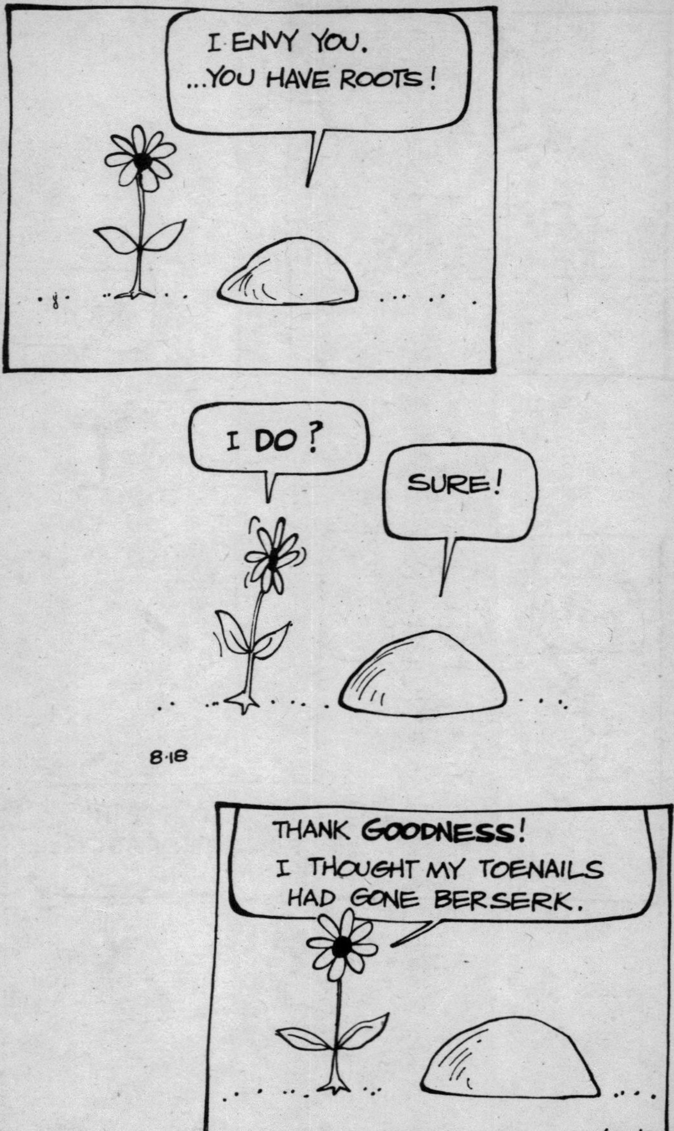
I ENVY YOU.
...YOU HAVE ROOTS!
I DO?
SURE!
8·18
THANK GOODNESS!
I THOUGHT MY TOENAILS HAD GONE BERSERK.
hart

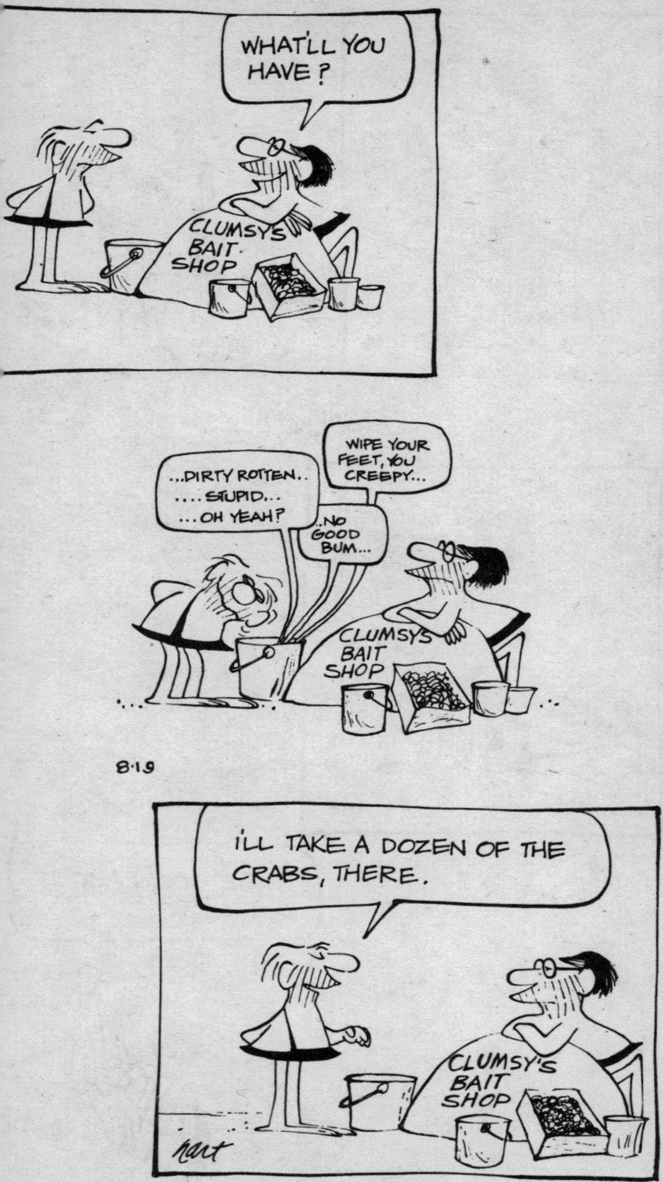
WHAT'LL YOU HAVE?
CLUMSY'S BAIT SHOP
...DIRTY ROTTEN.. .... STUPID... ...OH YEAH?
WIPE YOUR FEET, YOU CREEPY...
..NO GOOD BUM...
CLUMSY'S BAIT SHOP
8·19
I'LL TAKE A DOZEN OF THE CRABS, THERE.
CLUMSY'S BAIT SHOP
hart

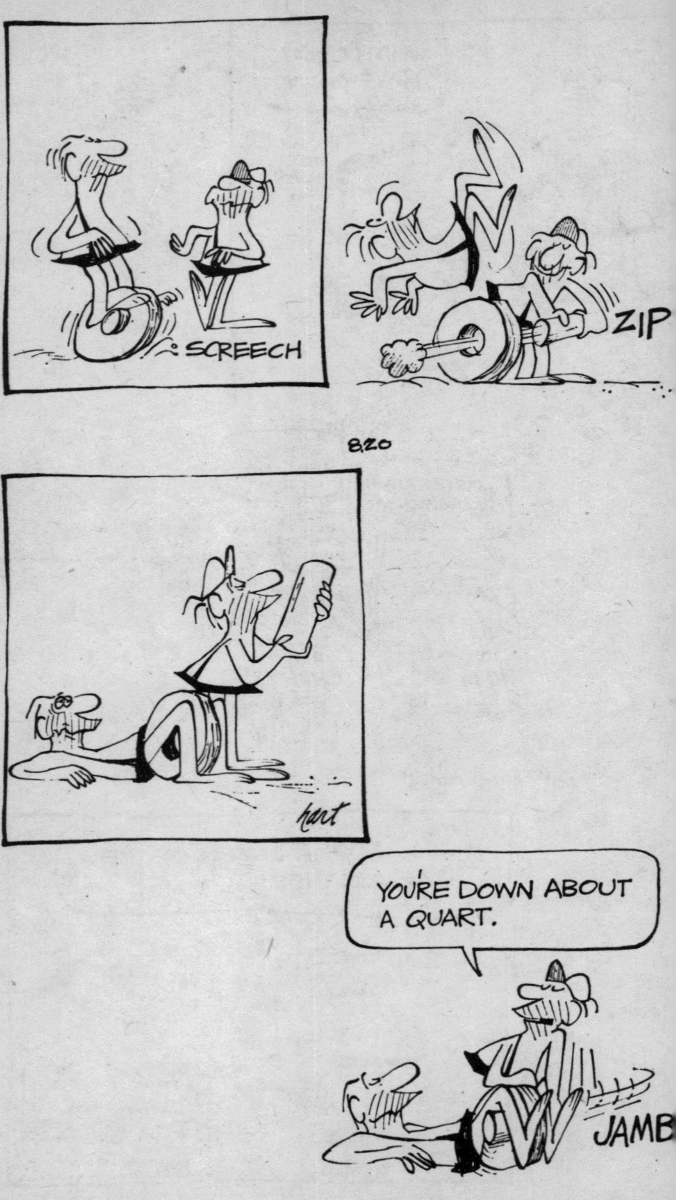
SCREECH
ZIP
8.20
hart
YOU'RE DOWN ABOUT A QUART.
JAMB

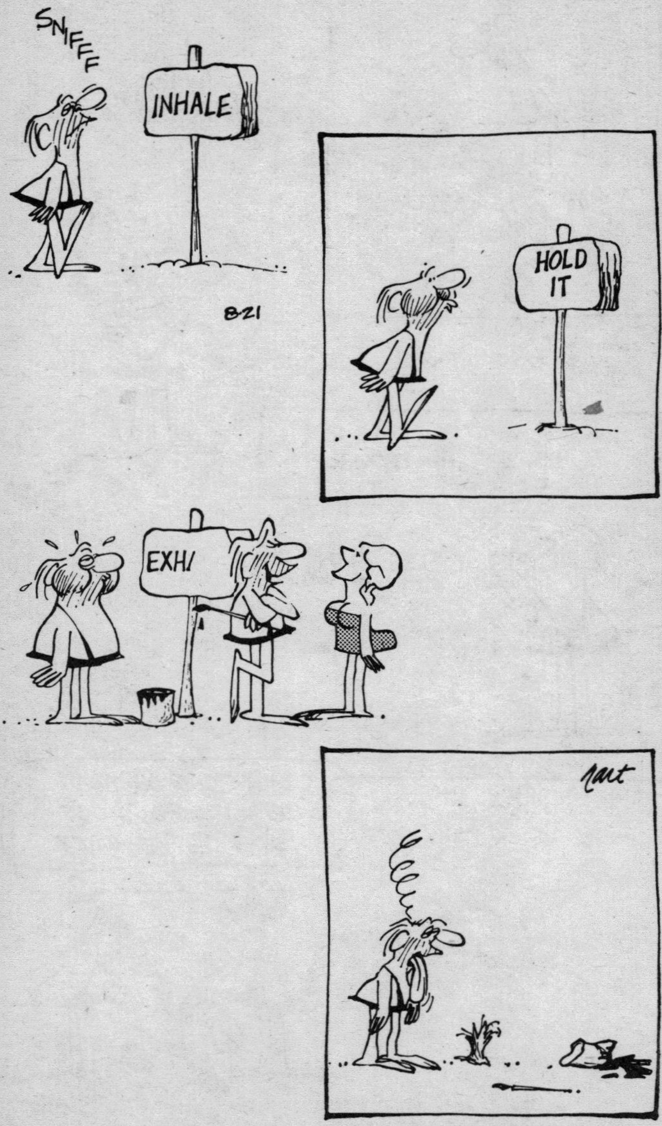
SNIFFF
INHALE
8-21
HOLD IT
EXH/
hart

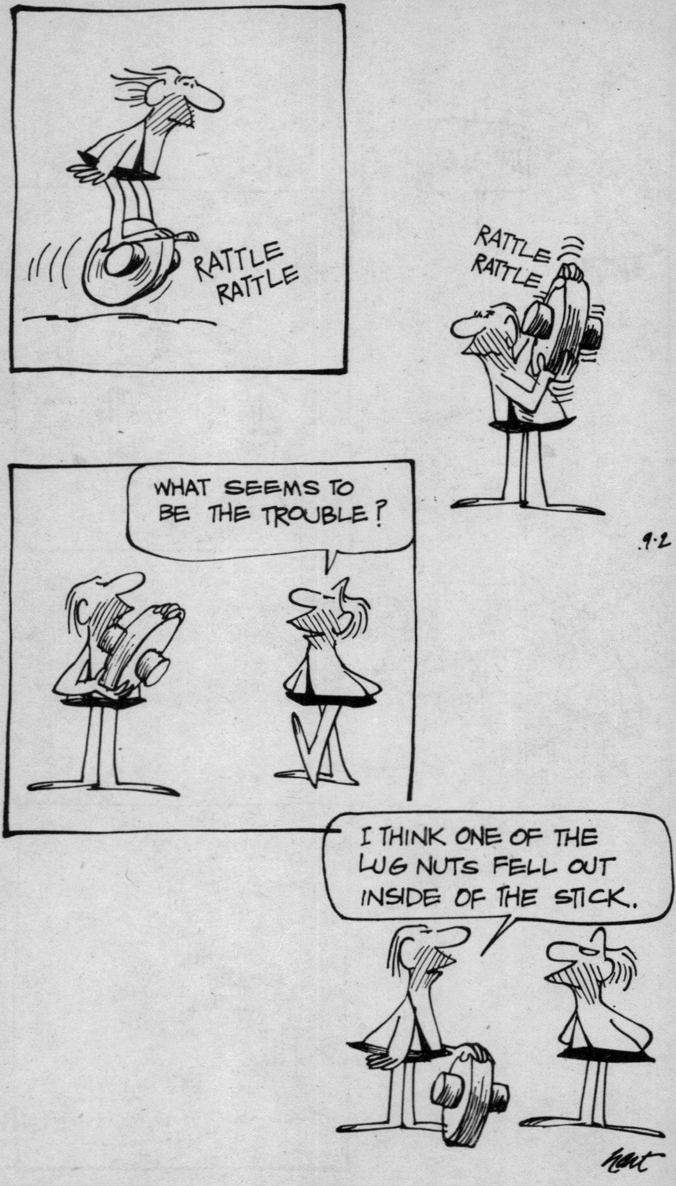
RATTLE
RATTLE
RATTLE
RATTLE
WHAT SEEMS TO BE THE TROUBLE?
I THINK ONE OF THE LUG NUTS FELL OUT INSIDE OF THE STICK.
9·2
hart

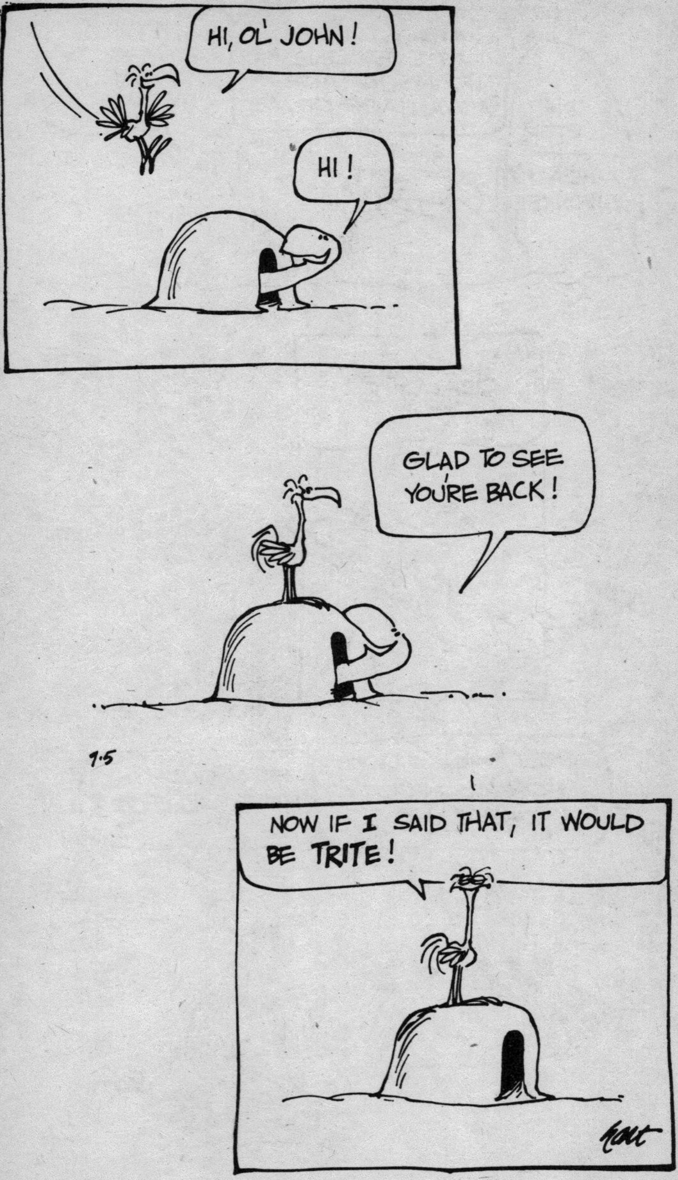
HI, OL' JOHN!
HI!
GLAD TO SEE YOU'RE BACK!
7-5
NOW IF I SAID THAT, IT WOULD BE TRITE!

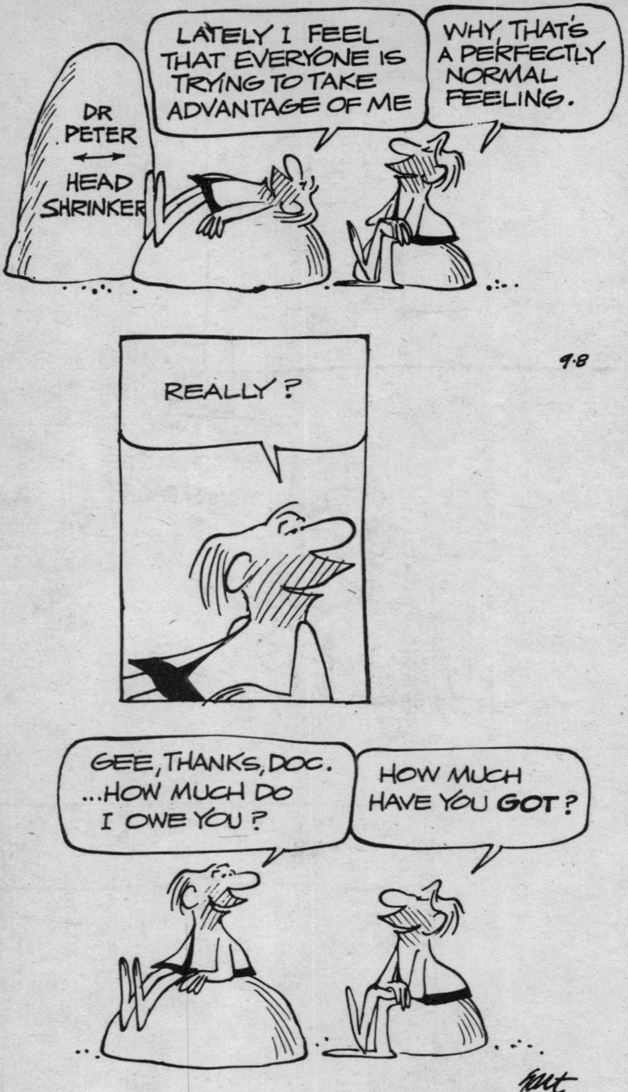
LATELY I FEEL THAT EVERYONE IS TRYING TO TAKE ADVANTAGE OF ME
WHY, THAT'S A PERFECTLY NORMAL FEELING.
DR PETER ⟷ HEAD SHRINKER
9·8
REALLY ?
GEE, THANKS, DOC. ...HOW MUCH DO I OWE YOU ?
HOW MUCH HAVE YOU **GOT** ?

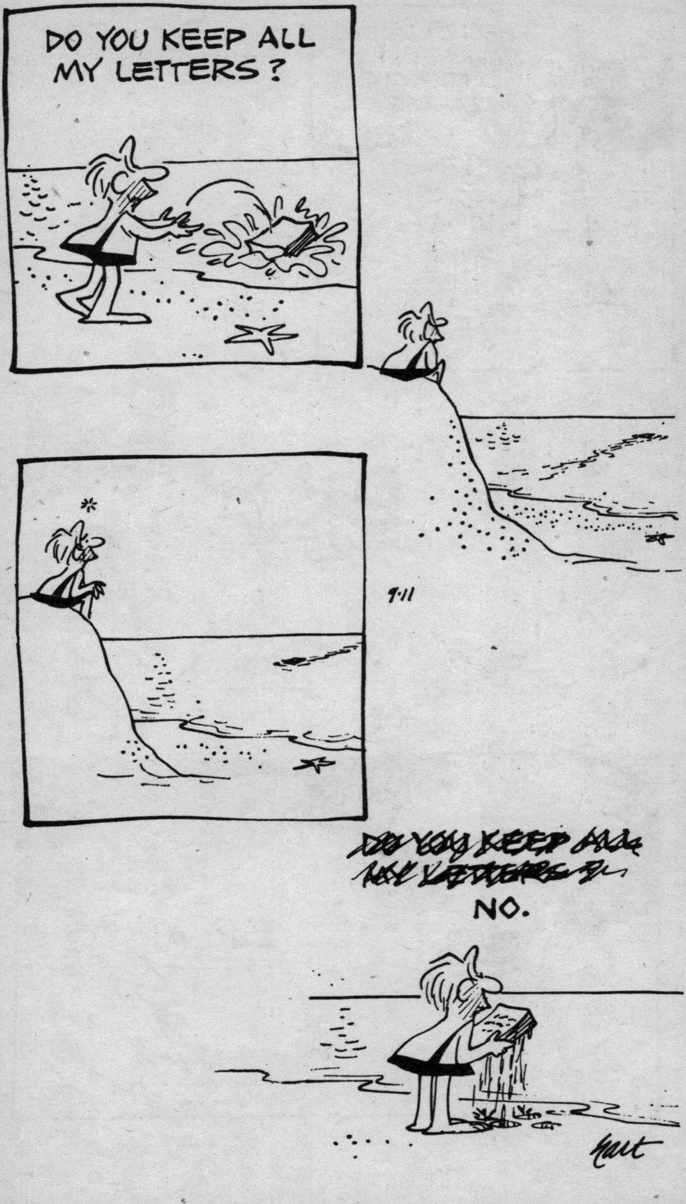

DO YOU KEEP ALL MY LETTERS?
9·11
NO.
hart

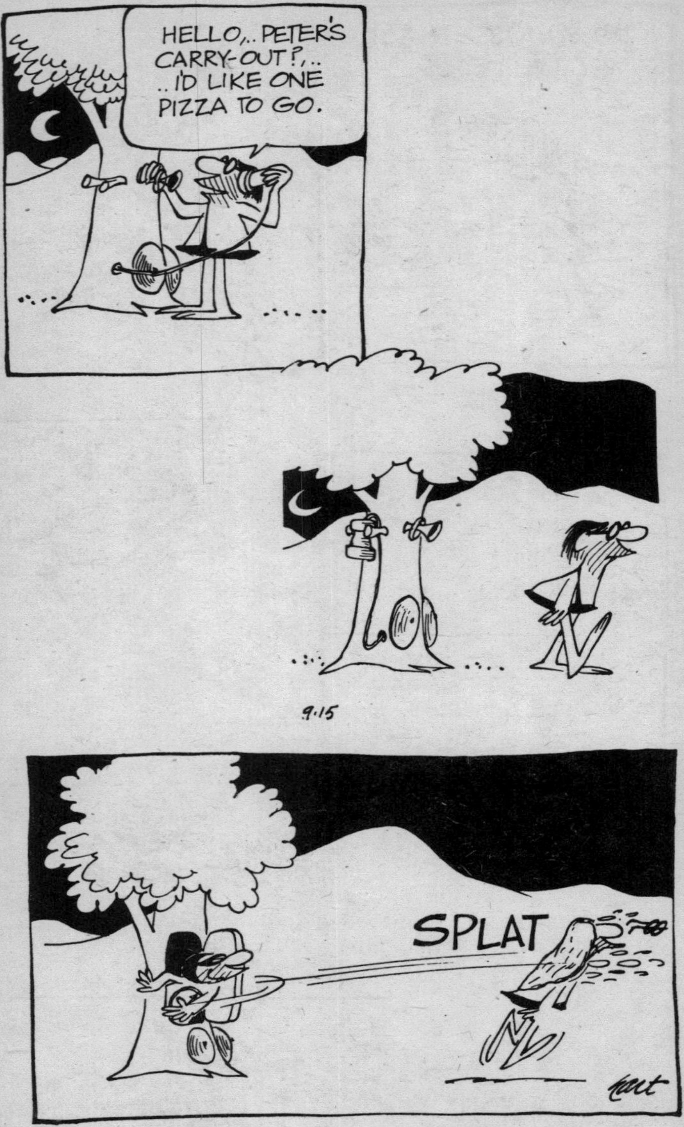
HELLO,.. PETER'S CARRY-OUT?,.. ..I'D LIKE ONE PIZZA TO GO.
9·15
SPLAT

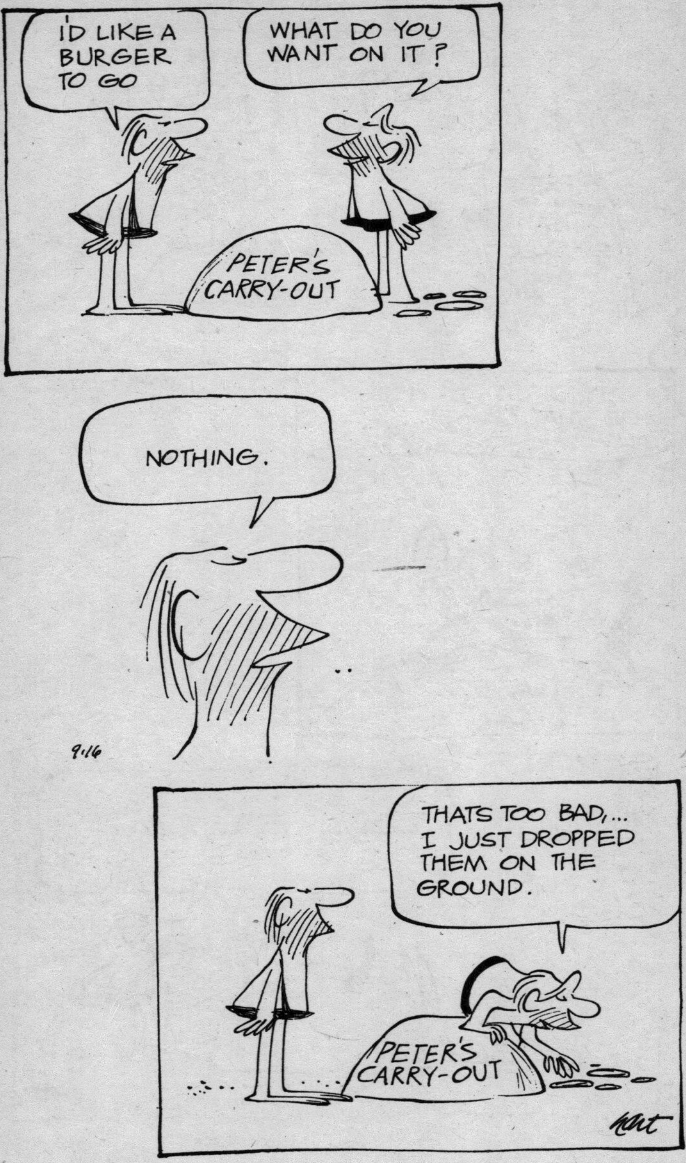
I'D LIKE A BURGER TO GO
WHAT DO YOU WANT ON IT?
PETER'S CARRY-OUT
NOTHING.
9·16
THATS TOO BAD,... I JUST DROPPED THEM ON THE GROUND.
PETER'S CARRY-OUT
hart

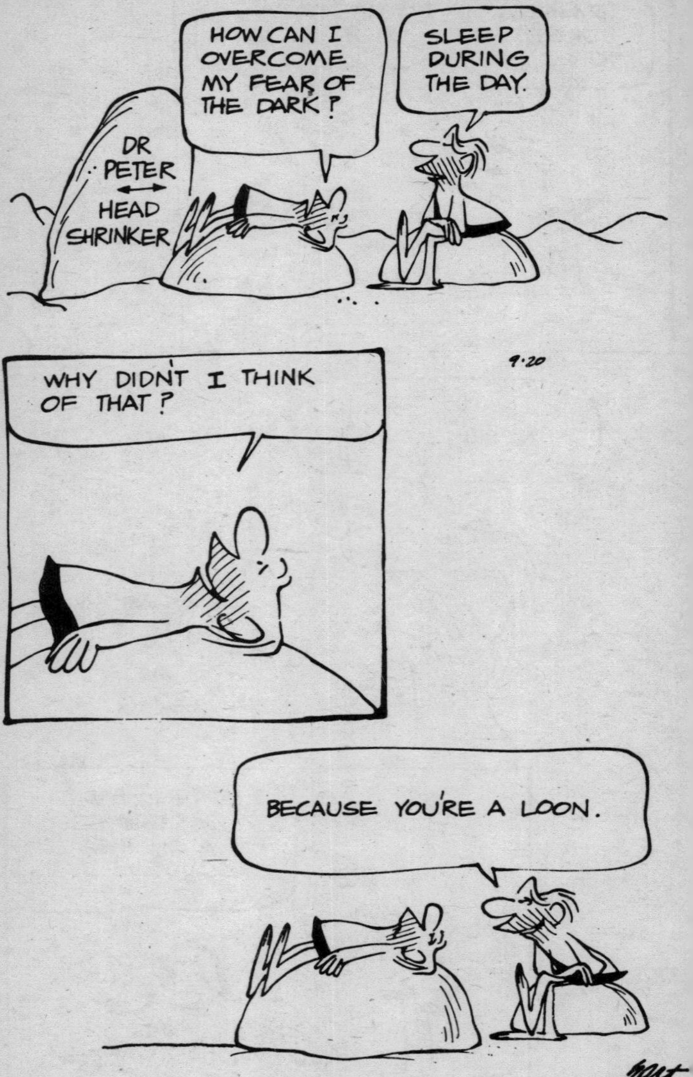
DR PETER ↔ HEAD SHRINKER
HOW CAN I OVERCOME MY FEAR OF THE DARK?
SLEEP DURING THE DAY.
WHY DIDN'T I THINK OF THAT?
9·20
BECAUSE YOU'RE A LOON.

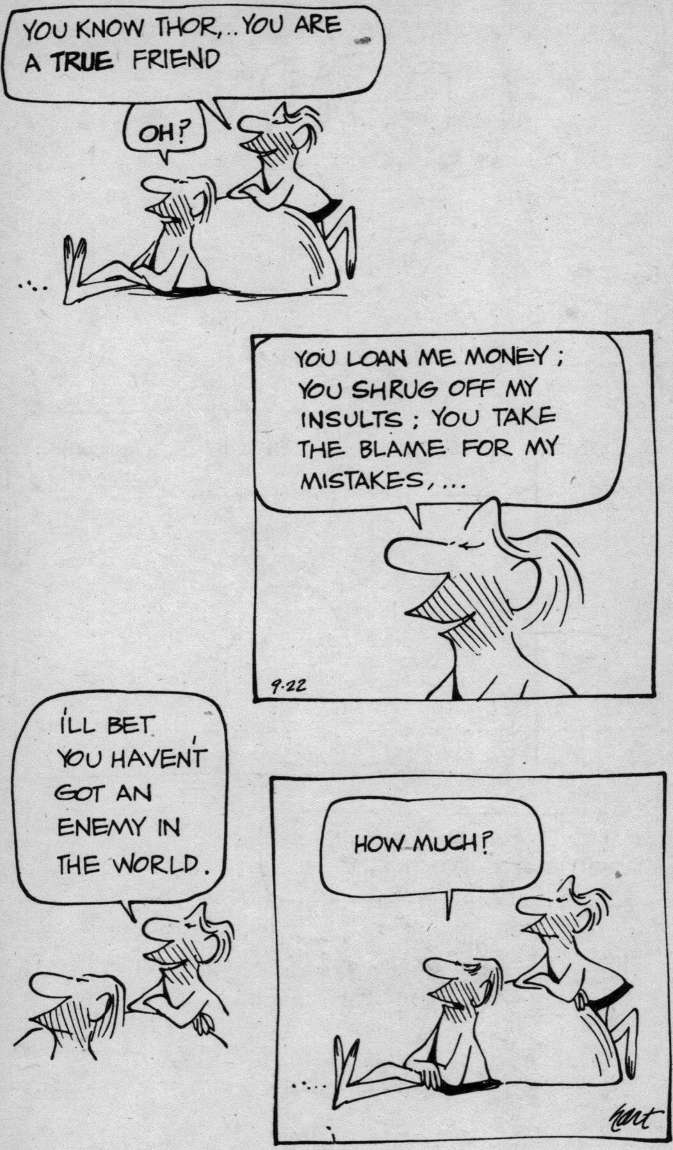
YOU KNOW THOR,.. YOU ARE A **TRUE** FRIEND
OH?
YOU LOAN ME MONEY; YOU SHRUG OFF MY INSULTS; YOU TAKE THE BLAME FOR MY MISTAKES,...
9·22
I'LL BET YOU HAVEN'T GOT AN ENEMY IN THE WORLD.
HOW MUCH?
hart

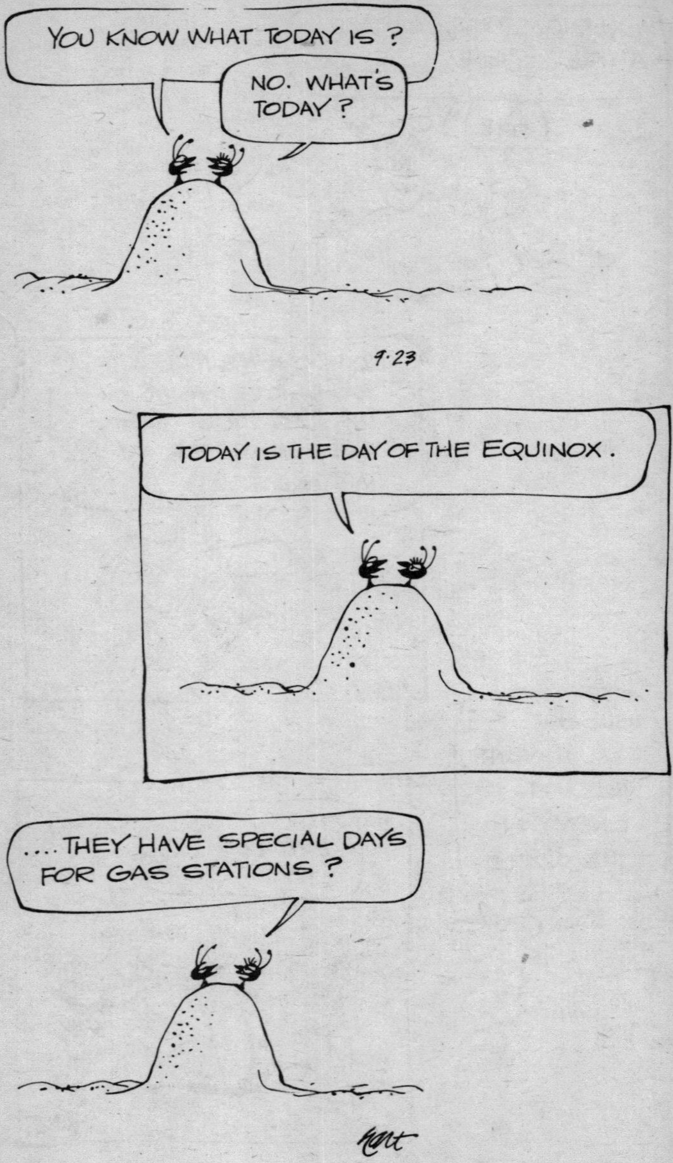
YOU KNOW WHAT TODAY IS ?
NO. WHAT'S TODAY ?
9·23
TODAY IS THE DAY OF THE EQUINOX .
.... THEY HAVE SPECIAL DAYS FOR GAS STATIONS ?
Hart

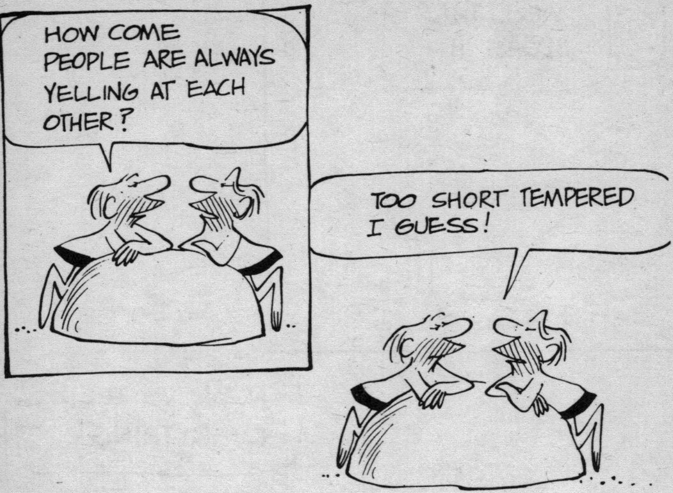
HOW COME PEOPLE ARE ALWAYS YELLING AT EACH OTHER?
TOO SHORT TEMPERED I GUESS!

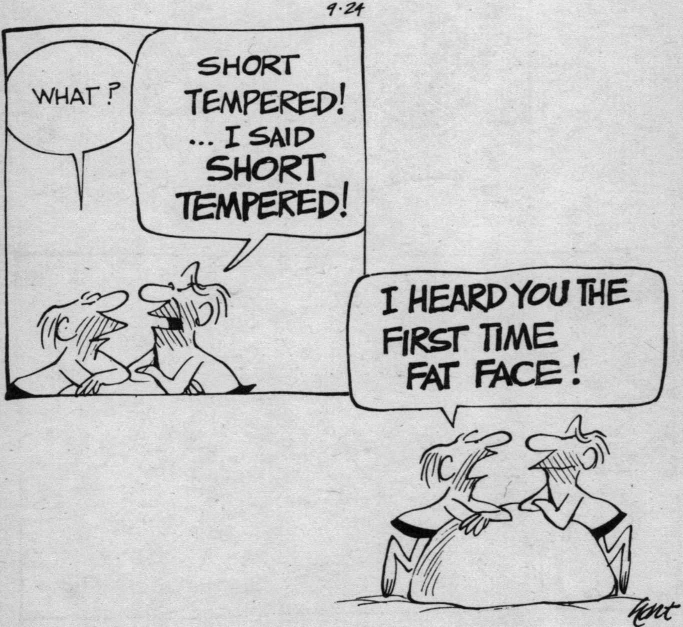
9·24
WHAT?
SHORT TEMPERED! ... I SAID SHORT TEMPERED!
I HEARD YOU THE FIRST TIME FAT FACE!

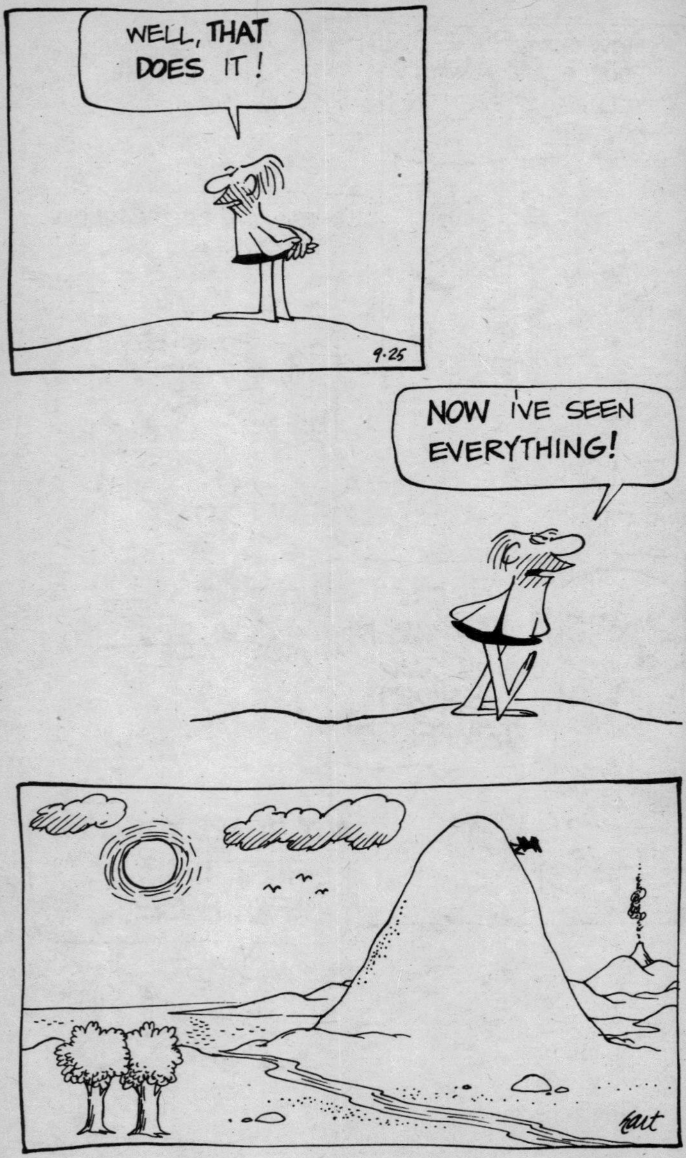
WELL, THAT DOES IT!
9·25
NOW I'VE SEEN EVERYTHING!

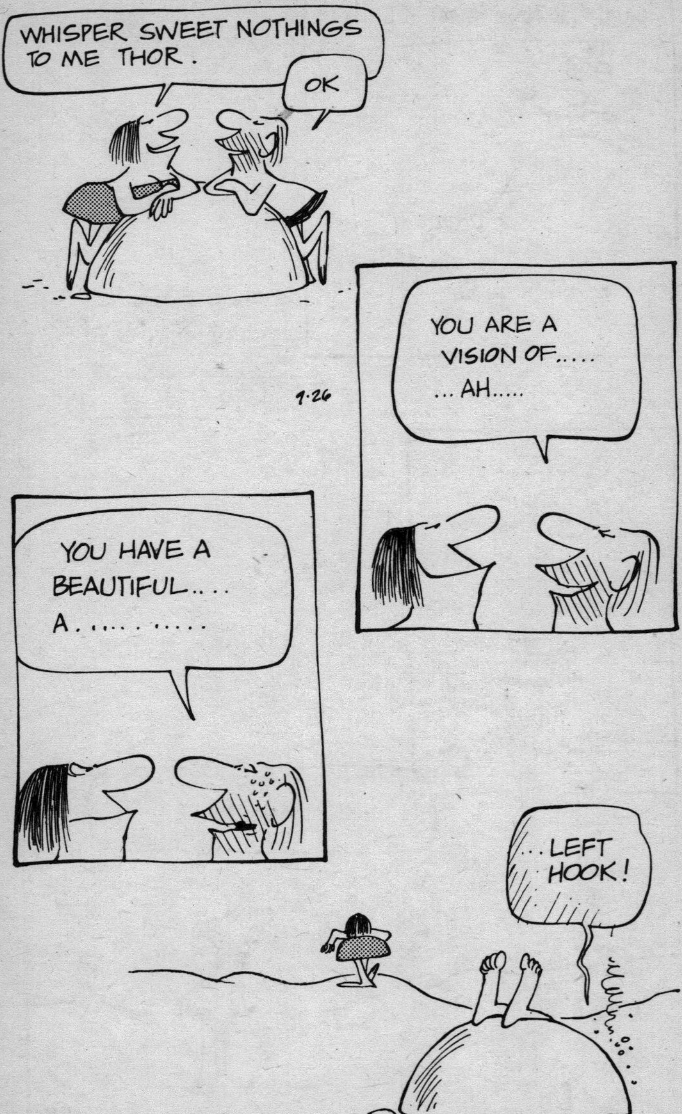
WHISPER SWEET NOTHINGS TO ME THOR.
OK
9·26
YOU ARE A VISION OF..... ...AH.....
YOU HAVE A BEAUTIFUL.... A.............
...LEFT HOOK!
hart

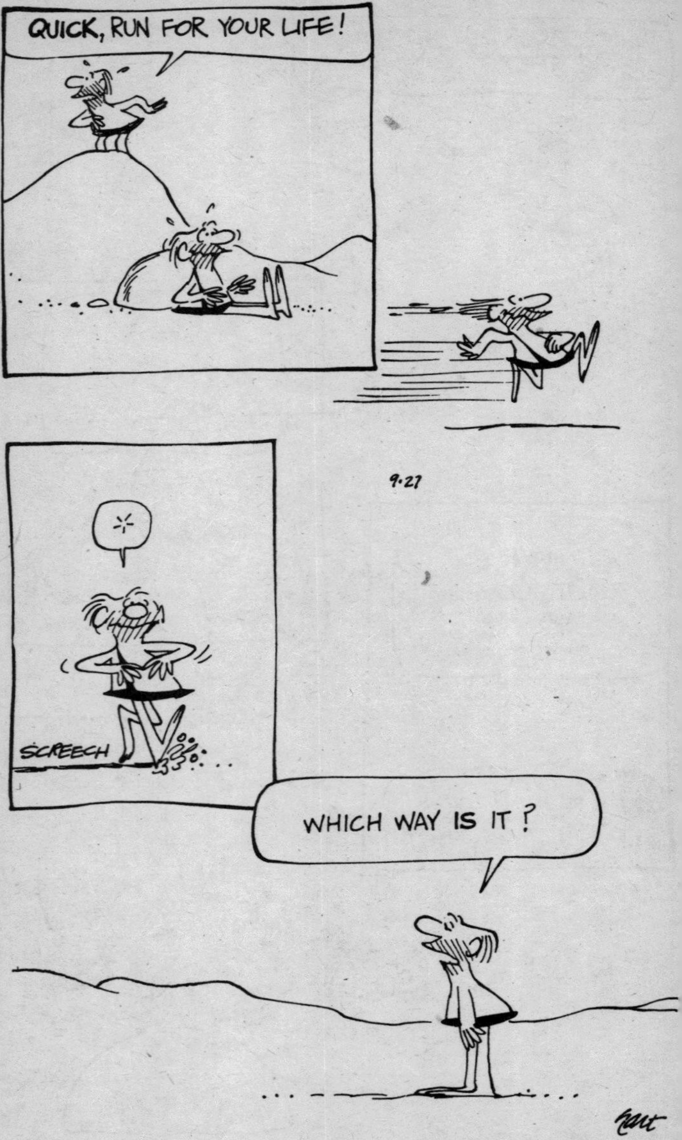
QUICK, RUN FOR YOUR LIFE!
SCREECH
WHICH WAY IS IT?
9-27

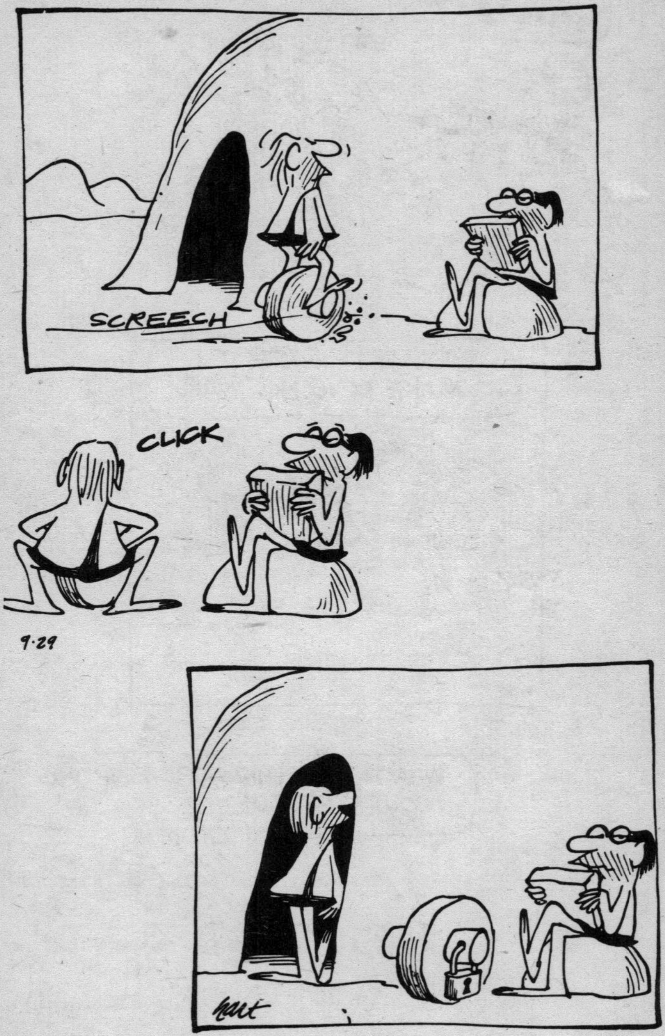
SCREECH
CLICK
9·29
hart

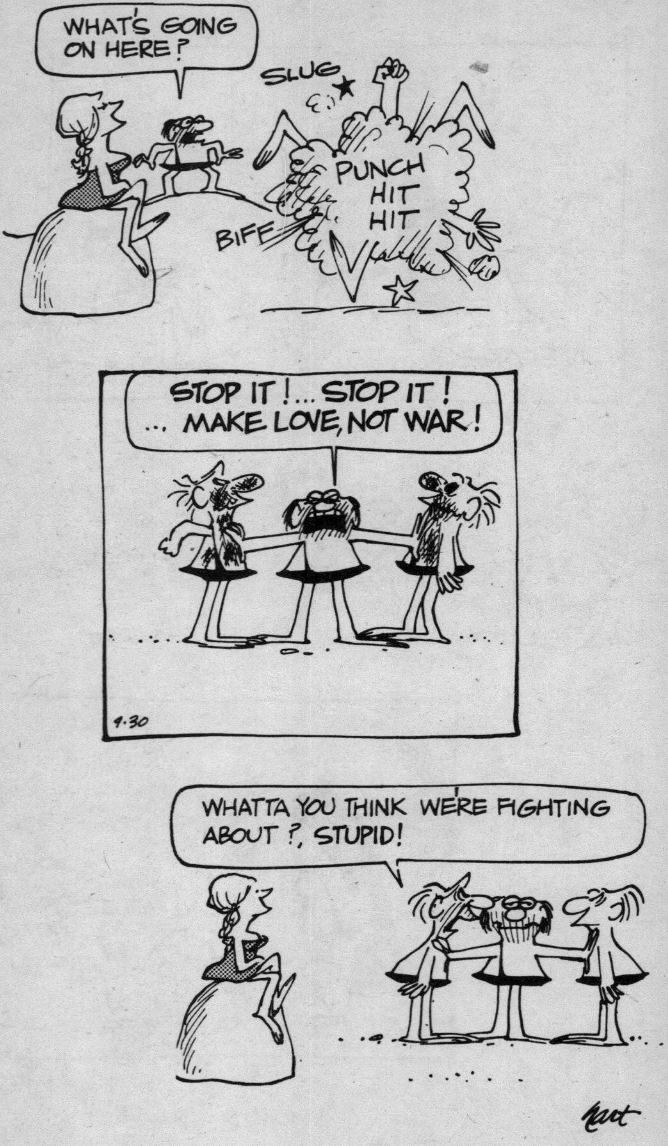

WHAT'S GOING ON HERE?
SLUG
PUNCH
HIT
HIT
BIFF
STOP IT!... STOP IT! ... MAKE LOVE, NOT WAR!
9·30
WHATTA YOU THINK WE'RE FIGHTING ABOUT?, STUPID!

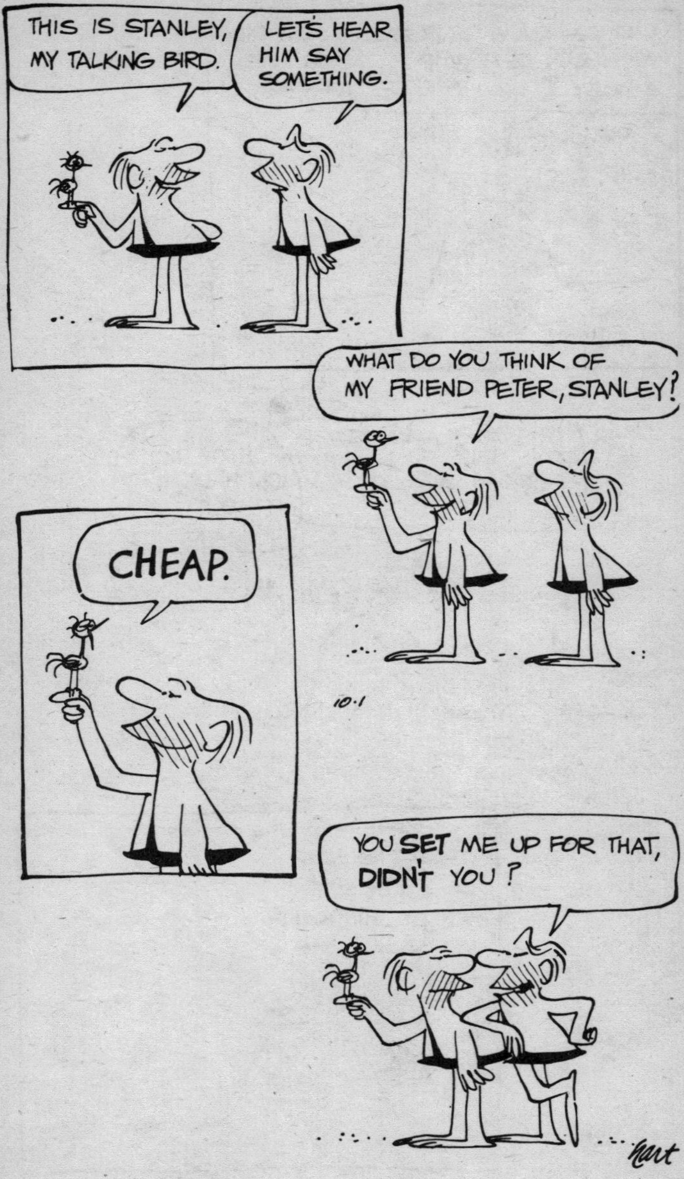
THIS IS STANLEY, MY TALKING BIRD.
LET'S HEAR HIM SAY SOMETHING.
WHAT DO YOU THINK OF MY FRIEND PETER, STANLEY?
10·1
CHEAP.
YOU SET ME UP FOR THAT, DIDN'T YOU?
hart

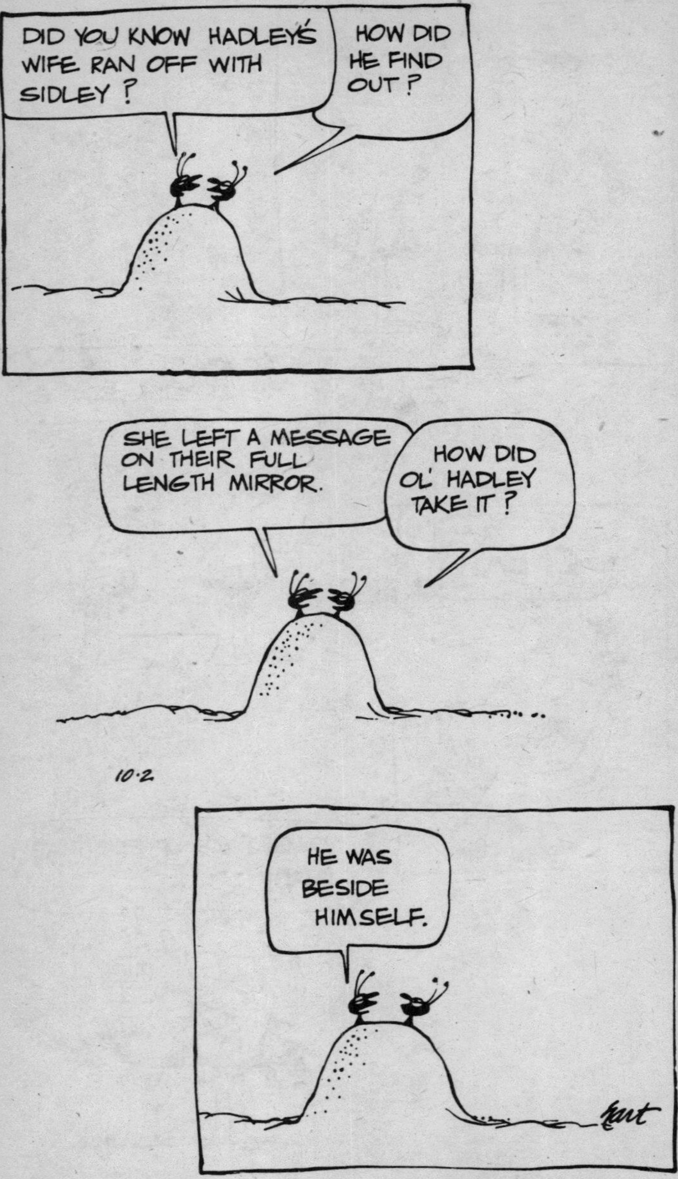
DID YOU KNOW HADLEY'S WIFE RAN OFF WITH SIDLEY?
HOW DID HE FIND OUT?
SHE LEFT A MESSAGE ON THEIR FULL LENGTH MIRROR.
HOW DID OL' HADLEY TAKE IT?
10·2
HE WAS BESIDE HIMSELF.
hart

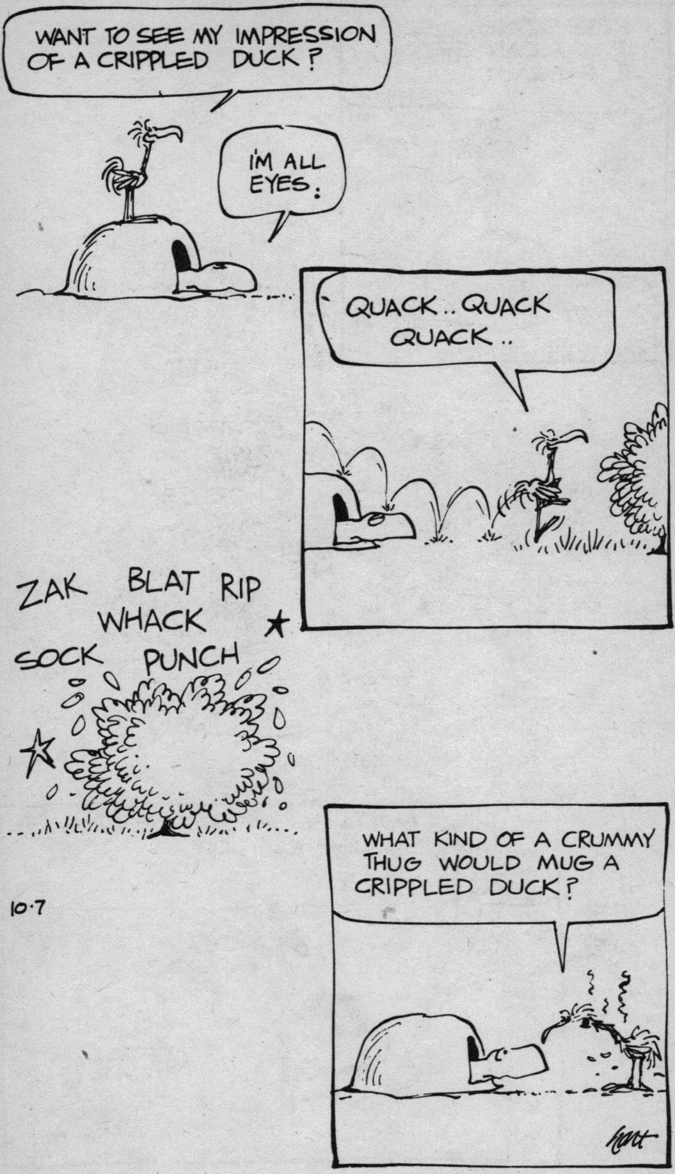

WANT TO SEE MY IMPRESSION OF A CRIPPLED DUCK?
I'M ALL EYES.
QUACK.. QUACK QUACK..
ZAK BLAT RIP WHACK SOCK PUNCH
10·7
WHAT KIND OF A CRUMMY THUG WOULD MUG A CRIPPLED DUCK?
hart

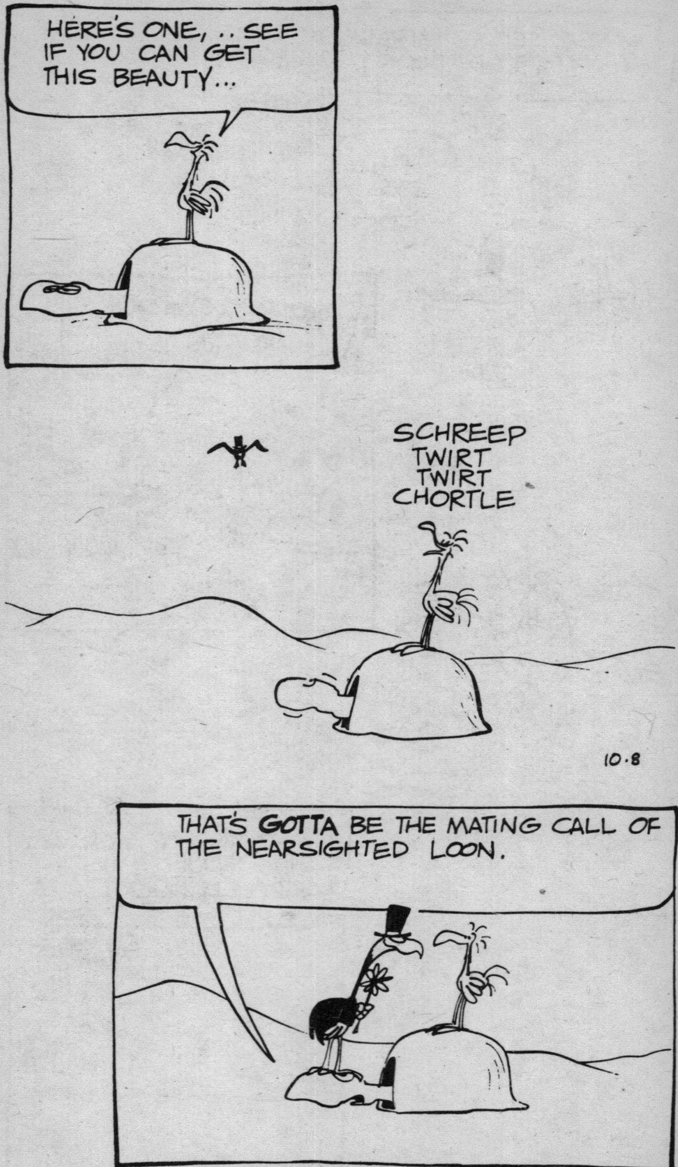
HERE'S ONE, .. SEE IF YOU CAN GET THIS BEAUTY...
SCHREEP TWIRT TWIRT CHORTLE
10·8
THAT'S **GOTTA** BE THE MATING CALL OF THE NEARSIGHTED LOON.

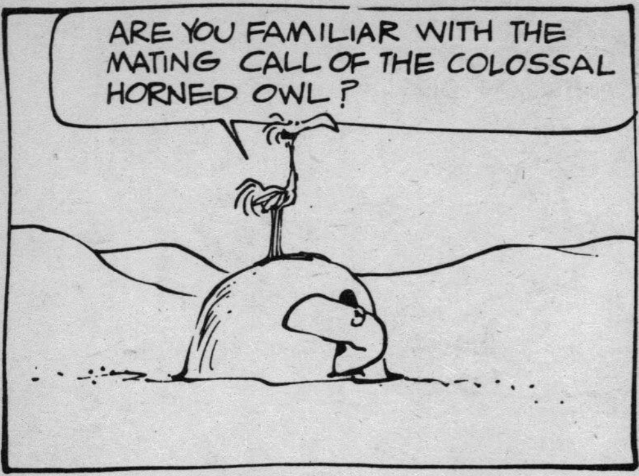
ARE YOU FAMILIAR WITH THE MATING CALL OF THE COLOSSAL HORNED OWL?

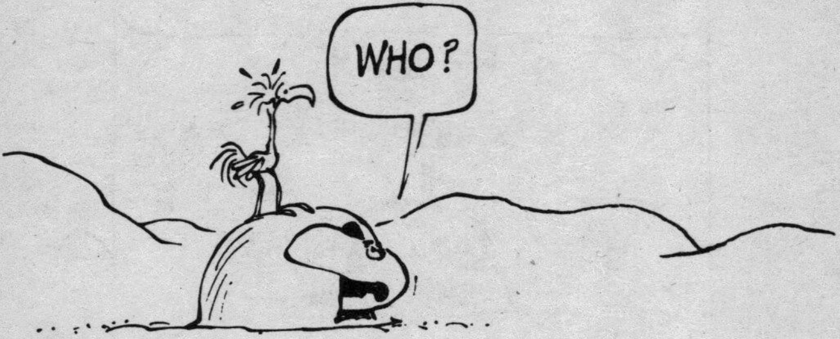
WHO?

10·9

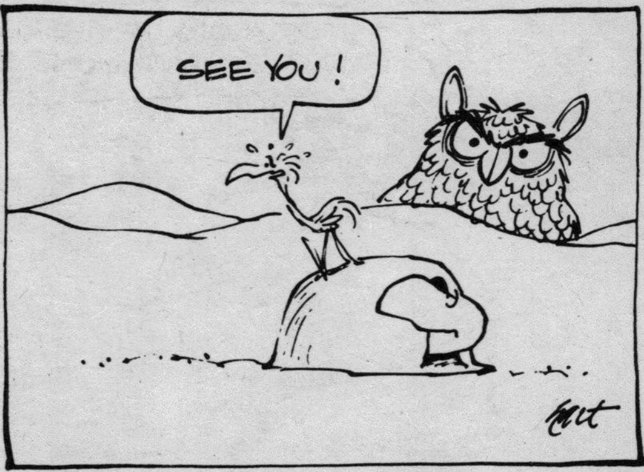
SEE YOU!

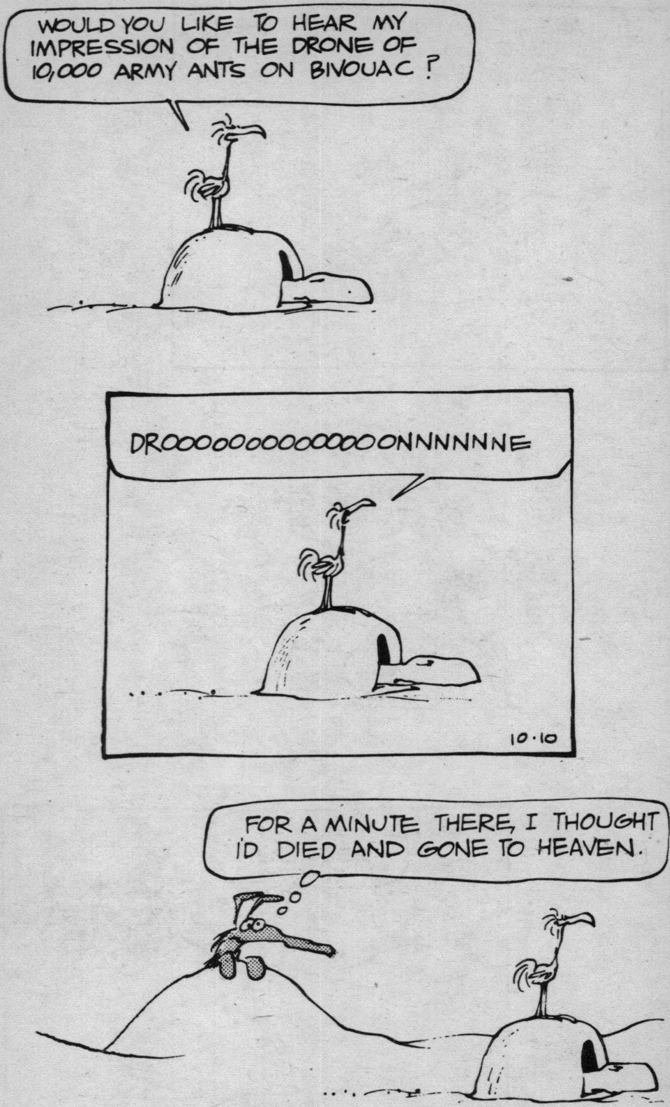
WOULD YOU LIKE TO HEAR MY IMPRESSION OF THE DRONE OF 10,000 ARMY ANTS ON BIVOUAC?
DROOOOOOOOOOOOOONNNNNNE
10·10
FOR A MINUTE THERE, I THOUGHT I'D DIED AND GONE TO HEAVEN.

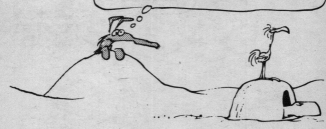

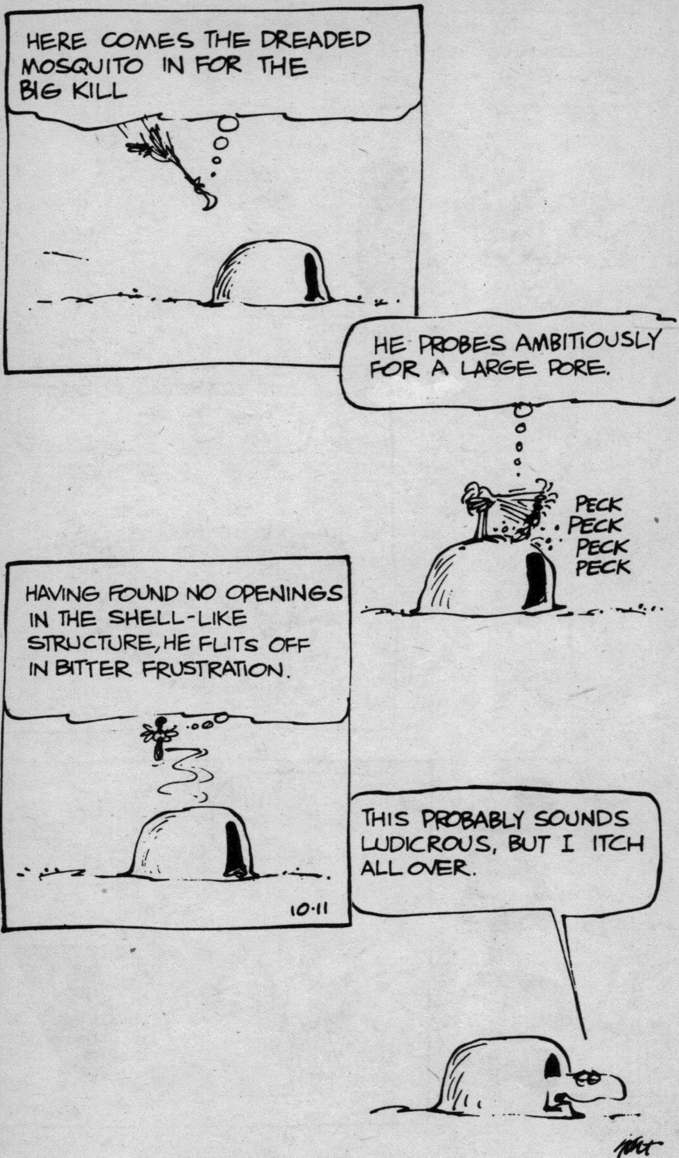
HERE COMES THE DREADED MOSQUITO IN FOR THE BIG KILL
HE PROBES AMBITIOUSLY FOR A LARGE PORE.
PECK PECK PECK PECK
HAVING FOUND NO OPENINGS IN THE SHELL-LIKE STRUCTURE, HE FLITS OFF IN BITTER FRUSTRATION.
10·11
THIS PROBABLY SOUNDS LUDICROUS, BUT I ITCH ALL OVER.

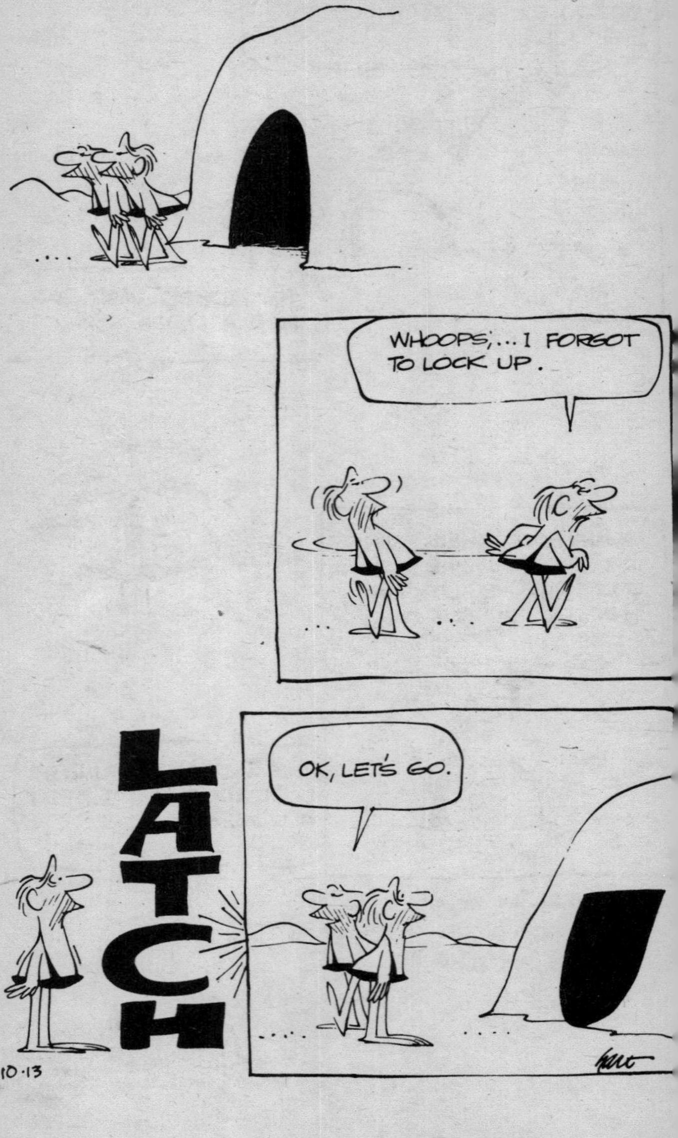
WHOOPS;... I FORGOT TO LOCK UP.
OK, LET'S GO.
LATCH
10·13

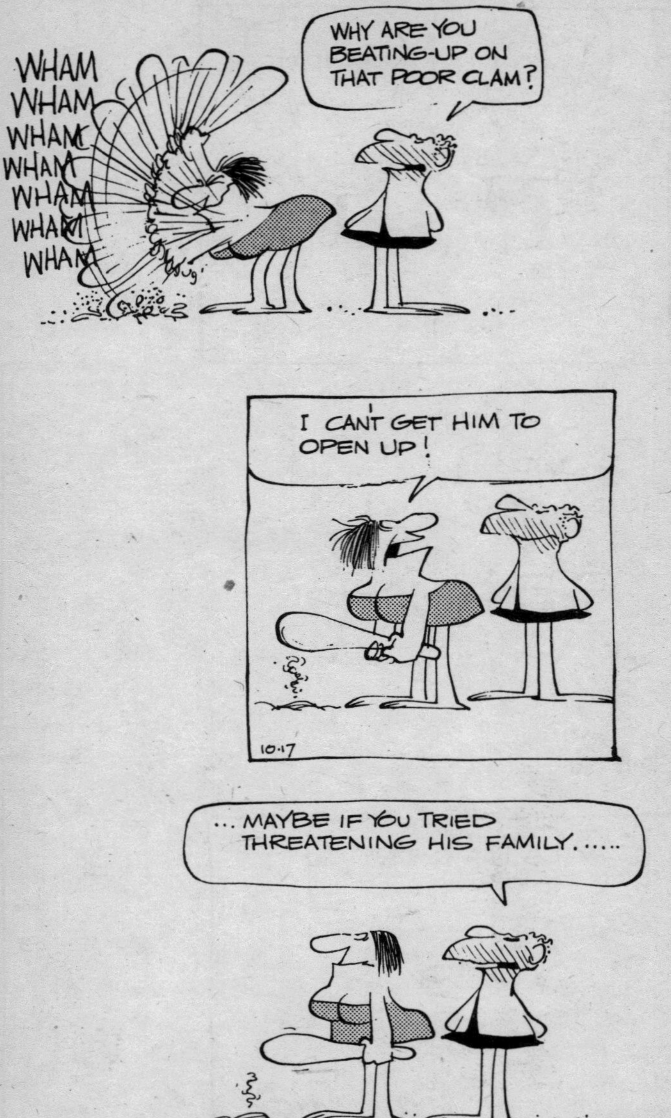
WHY ARE YOU BEATING-UP ON THAT POOR CLAM?
WHAM WHAM WHAM WHAM WHAM WHAM WHAM
I CAN'T GET HIM TO OPEN UP!
10·17
... MAYBE IF YOU TRIED THREATENING HIS FAMILY.....

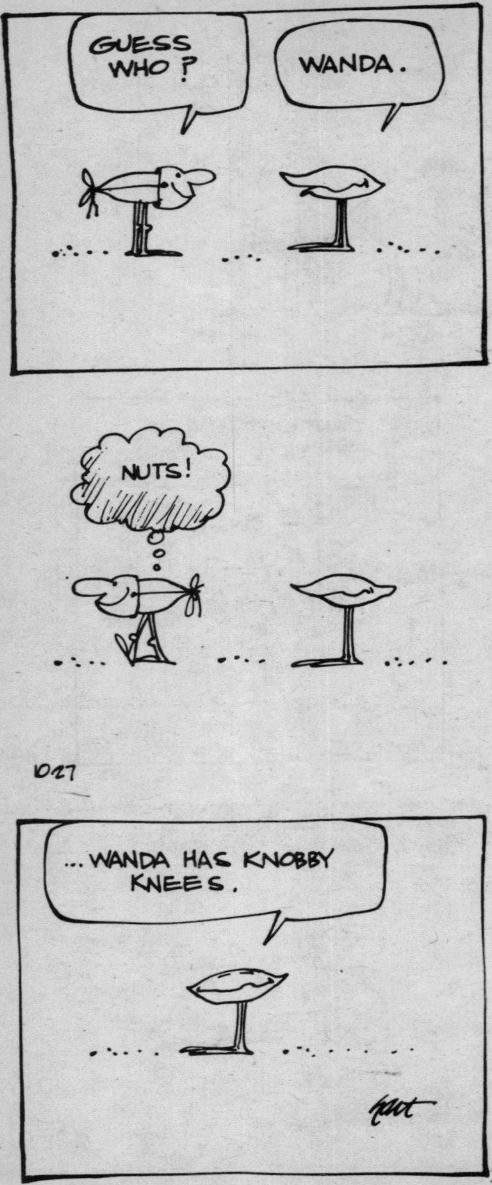
GUESS WHO?
WANDA.
NUTS!
...WANDA HAS KNOBBY KNEES.

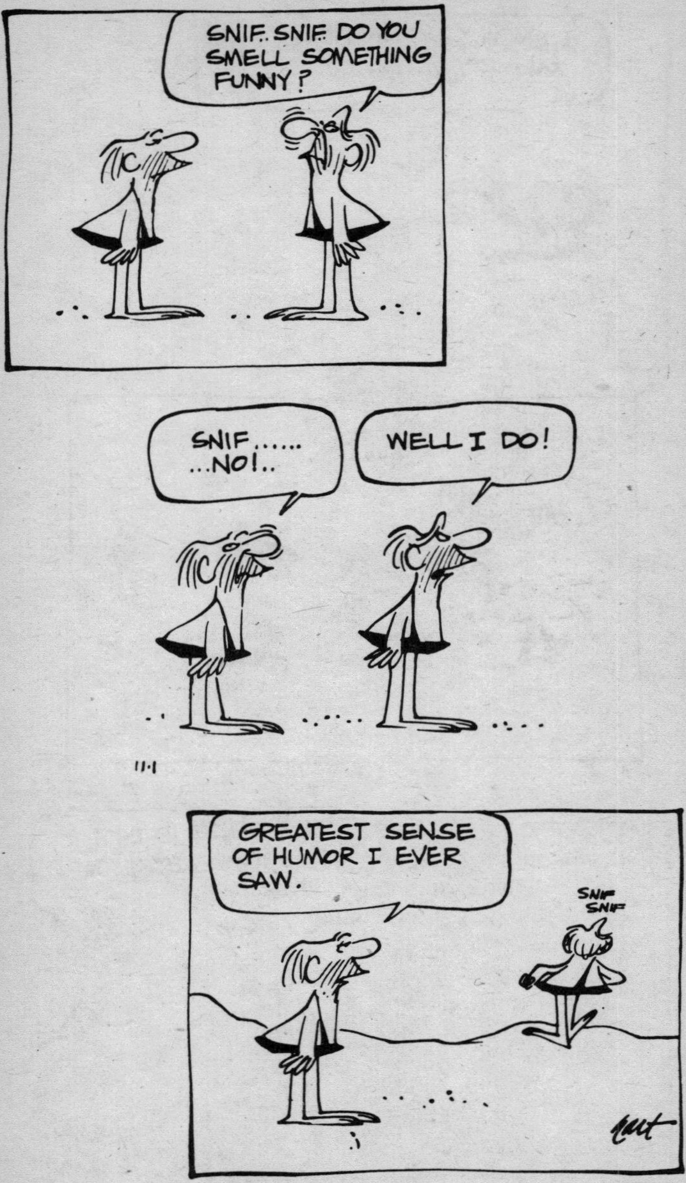
SNIF.. SNIF.. DO YOU SMELL SOMETHING FUNNY?
SNIF...... ...NO!..
WELL I DO!
GREATEST SENSE OF HUMOR I EVER SAW.
SNIF SNIF

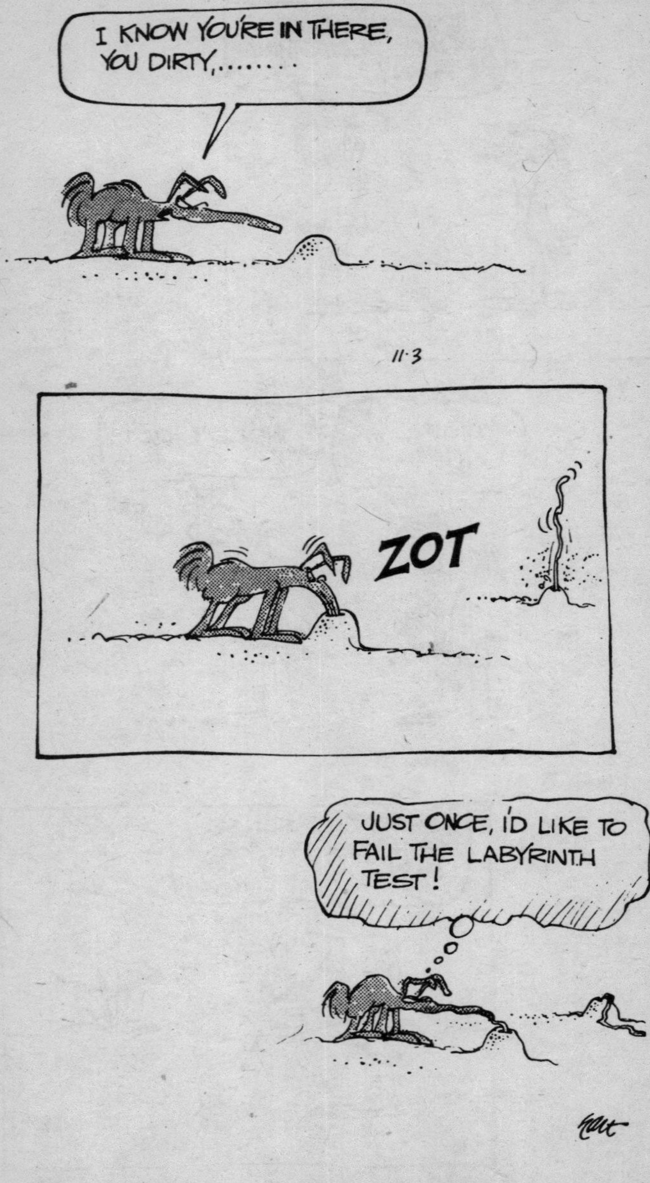
I KNOW YOU'RE IN THERE, YOU DIRTY,.......
11·3
ZOT
JUST ONCE, I'D LIKE TO FAIL THE LABYRINTH TEST!

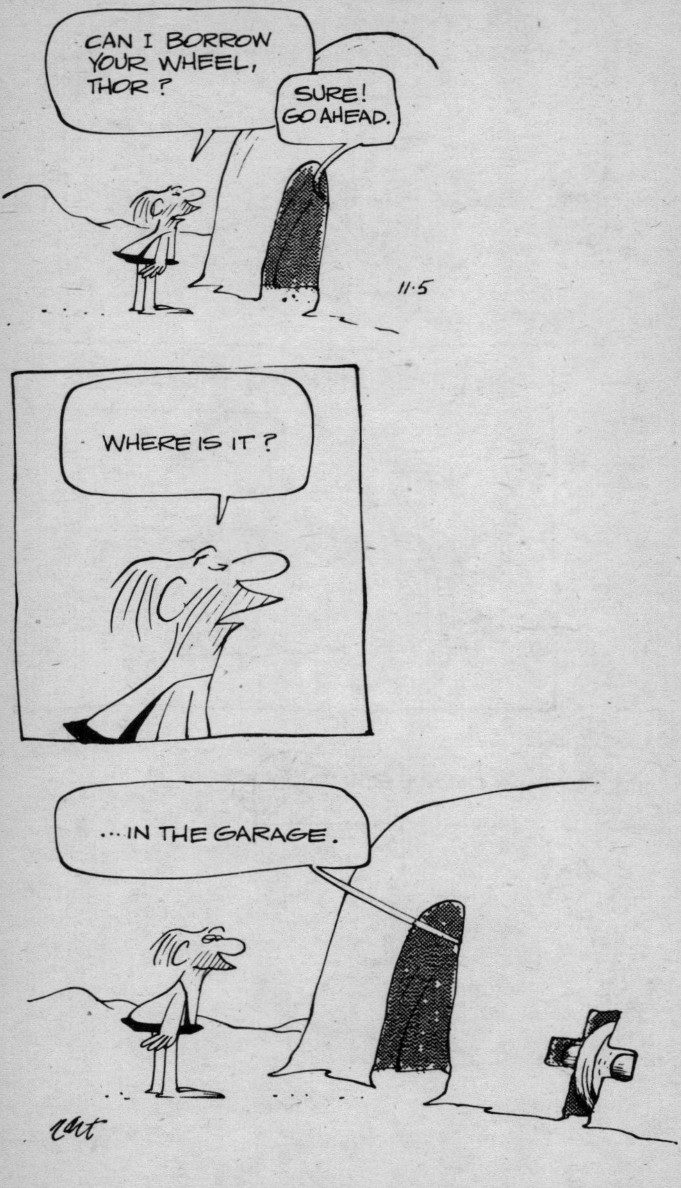
CAN I BORROW YOUR WHEEL, THOR?
SURE! GO AHEAD.
11·5
WHERE IS IT?
...IN THE GARAGE.
tait

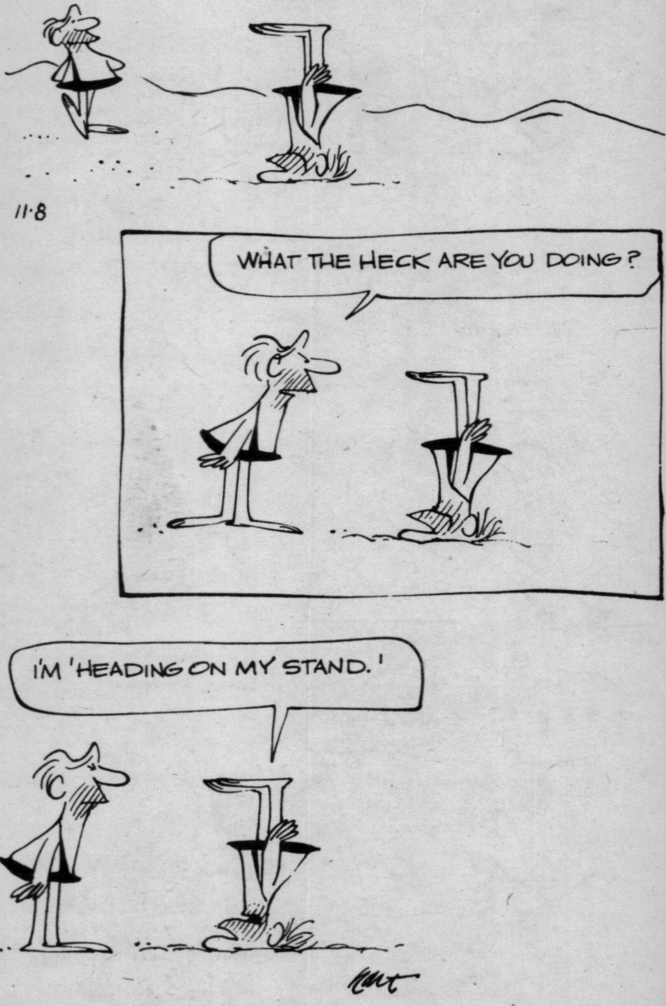
11·8
WHAT THE HECK ARE YOU DOING?
I'M 'HEADING ON MY STAND.'
hart

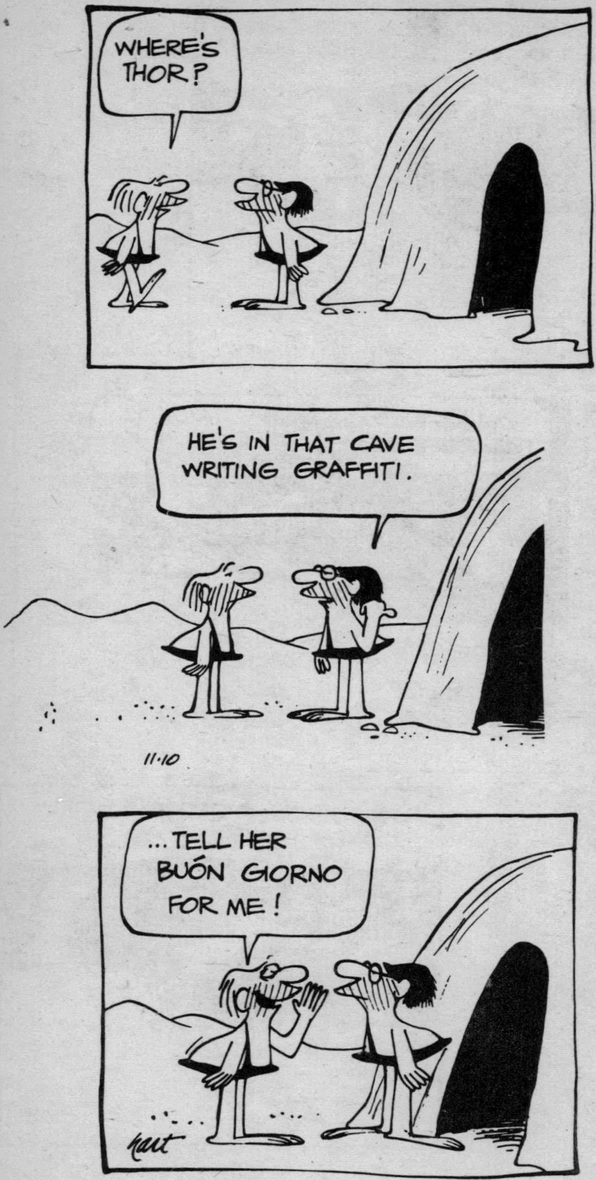
WHERE'S THOR?
HE'S IN THAT CAVE WRITING GRAFFITI.
11·10
...TELL HER BUÓN GIORNO FOR ME!
hart

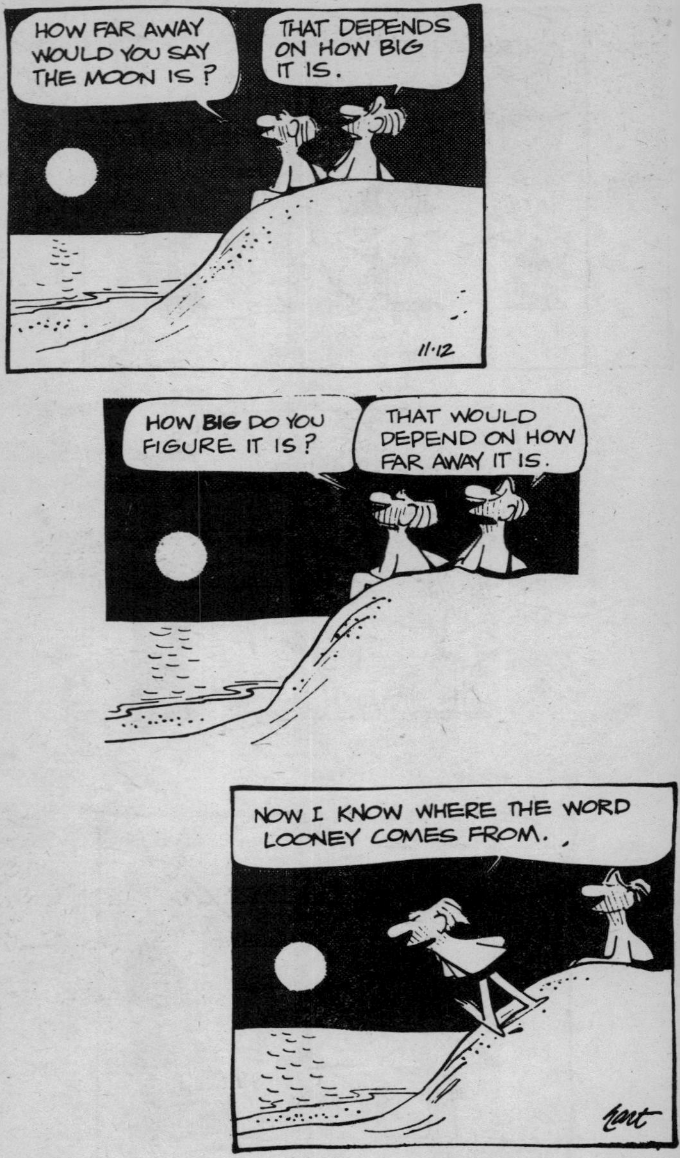
HOW FAR AWAY WOULD YOU SAY THE MOON IS?
THAT DEPENDS ON HOW BIG IT IS.
11·12
HOW BIG DO YOU FIGURE IT IS?
THAT WOULD DEPEND ON HOW FAR AWAY IT IS.
NOW I KNOW WHERE THE WORD LOONEY COMES FROM.
hart

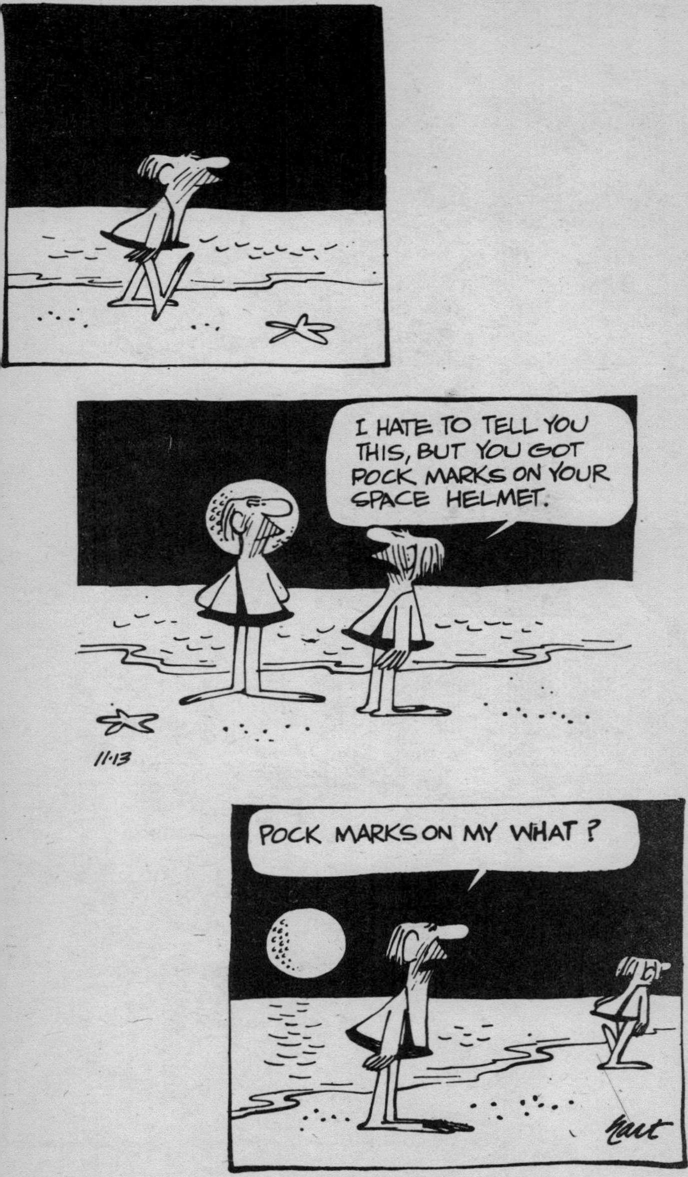
I HATE TO TELL YOU THIS, BUT YOU GOT POCK MARKS ON YOUR SPACE HELMET.
11·13
POCK MARKS ON MY WHAT ?
Hart